The Popular Carol Book

MOWBRAY

Introduction

Carols are songs that people have enjoyed singing to celebrate the festivals and seasons of the Christian year. They are essentially popular songs rather than liturgical music, and have been sung in the streets, inside and outside homes, in schools and halls as well as in churches. Originally they accompanied dancing too. This collection draws on carols from many countries and traditions and includes all the well-known favourites.

It is a people's carol book that does not attempt to compete with the many collections of carols for choirs. It has a wide range of carols for Advent, Christmas and Epiphany and includes many recent carols that broadcasts have made popular. It also includes carols that have become popular in schools and is a collection to be enjoyed by carol singers of all ages.

Most of the well-known carols appear in their traditional form. Inclusive language has been incorporated where possible, especially in translations and in modern carols.

The music is arranged for keyboard, or guitar, but additional accompaniments may be added for whatever combination of instruments is available to accompany the carolling. The notes for each carol give directions for the music where this is helpful, as well as providing the background to the words.

Many of the carols simply tell the Christmas story. Others reflect on particular themes, and some express rather more Christian commitment. This collection gives a wide enough choice to be able to be used as the people's carol book on every occasion. Carols are part of the fun of Christmas: joining in the singing becomes a way of sharing in the joy.

Patrick Appleford
Elizabeth Barr
Richard Coleman
Geoffrey Court
Ruth McCurry
Rosalind Russell

1 *A child this day is born* Sandys

1. A child this day is born,
   A child of high renown;
   Most worthy of a sceptre,
   A sceptre and a crown.

2. Good news the shepherds heard,
   Who watched their flock and fold;
   The angel that appeared to them
   Of God's salvation told.

3. And what the angel said,
   Did yet in truth appear;
   At Bethlehem they found the child,
   Laid in a manger there.

4. Then glory be to God
   Who reigns supreme on high;
   With glad thanksgiving, worthy praise,
   And joyful melody!

5. Nowell, nowell, nowell,
   Nowell sing all we may,
   Because the King of all kings
   Was born on Christmas day.

*The original words came, like the tune, from
William Sandys's* Christmas Carols, *published in 1833.
Our version is somewhat shorter than the 21 verses
included there.*

English traditional

2. A cry in the night (Ballad of the Homeless Christ) Notting Hill

1. A cry in the night
   And a child is born;
   A child in a stable,
   There isn't any room:
   A cry in the night, and God has made
   Our homelessness his home.

2. A trial in the dark,
   The disciples run;
   They bring him to Pilate,
   He stands there all alone:
   A trial in the dark, and God has made
   Our homelessness his home.

3. A man on a cross,
   And the sun beats down;
   Up there on the gallows
   He's got a thorny crown:
   A man on a cross, and God has made
   Our homelessness his home.

4. A voice in the dawn
   When the women came;
   'You're looking for Jesus,
   Don't seek him in a tomb':
   A voice in the dawn, and God has made
   Our homelessness his home.

A carol with an explicit social message about homelessness, arising out of the very poor housing situation, particularly for black families, in Geoffrey Ainger's Notting Hill parish during the 1960s. It relates to all homeless people everywhere.
   'Notting Hill' was composed by Ian Calvert (b. 1940), a member of the same church.

Geoffrey Ainger (b. 1925)

Words and music © Geoffrey Ainger. Used by permission of Stainer and Bell.
USA © 1964, Galliard Ltd. Used by permission of Galaxy Music Corp., Boston.

3. A great and mighty wonder
Es Ist Ein Ros' Entsprungen

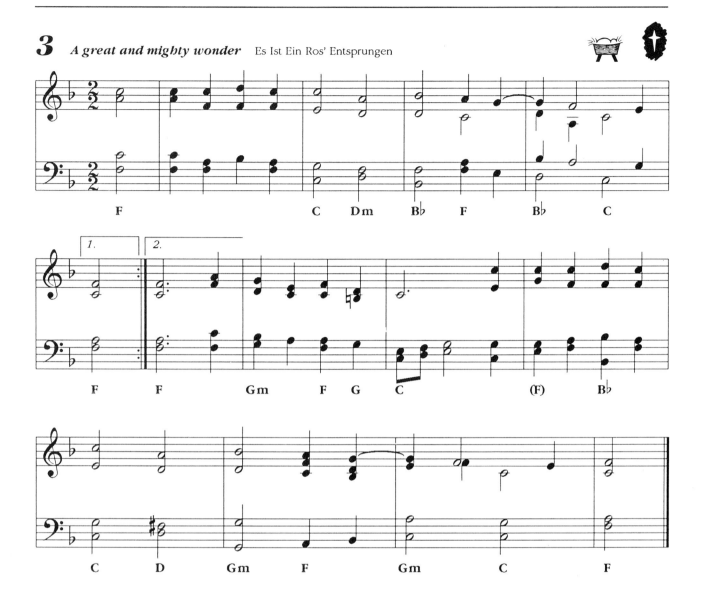

1 A great and mighty wonder,
   A full and holy cure!
   The Virgin bears the Infant
   With virgin-honour pure.

   Repeat the hymn again!
   'To God on high be glory,
   And peace on earth shall reign!'

2 The word becomes incarnate
   And yet remains on high!
   And cherubim sing anthems
   To shepherds from the sky.

   Repeat the hymn again! . . .

3 While thus they sing your Monarch,
   Those bright angelic bands,
   Rejoice, ye vales and mountains,
   Ye oceans clap your hands.

   Repeat the hymn again! . . .

4 Since all he comes to ransom,
   By all be he adored,
   The Infant born in Bethl'em,
   The Saviour and the Lord.

   Repeat the hymn again! . . .

5 And idol forms shall perish,
   And error shall decay,
   And Christ shall wield his sceptre,
   Our Lord and God for ay.

   Repeat the hymn again! . . .

A German traditional carol, whose melody, harmonized by Michael Praetorius (1571–1621), is full of rhythmic interest, and needs a dancing lightness in performance.

St Germanus (634 – 734), tr. John Mason Neale (1818–66)

4 All my heart this night rejoices — Bonn

1. All my heart this night rejoices
   As I hear,
   Far and near,
   Sweetest angel voices:
   'Christ is born!' their choirs are singing,
   Till the air
   Ev'rywhere
   Now with joy is ringing.

2. Hark! a voice from yonder manger,
   Soft and sweet,
   Doth entreat,
   'Flee from woe and danger!
   People, come! from all doth grieve you,
   You are freed;
   All you need
   I will surely give you.'

3. Come, then, let us hasten yonder!
   Here let all,
   Great and small,
   Kneel in awe and wonder!
   Love him who with love is yearning!
   Hail the star
   That from far
   Bright with hope is burning!

4. Thee, dear Lord, with heed I'll cherish,
   Live to thee,
   And with thee,
   Dying, shall not perish;
   But shall dwell with thee for ever,
   Far on high,
   In the joy
   That can alter never.

Lutheran Paul Gerhardt lived for the whole of his youth and early adulthood through the Thirty Years War. His many great hymns, with their mystical quality, strike a personal note. In this one we are all called to the manger.
'Bonn', by Johann Georg Ebeling (1637–76), is of very simple construction, a pre-Bach chorale making a marvellous congregational anthem.

Paul Gerhardt (1607–76),
tr. Catherine Winkworth (1829–78)

1 Angels, from the realms of glory,
   Wing your flight o'er all the earth;
   Ye who sang creation's story,
   Now proclaim Messiah's birth:

   Come and worship
   Christ the new-born King;
   Come and worship,
   Worship Christ, the new-born King.

2 Shepherds, in the field abiding,
   Watching o'er your flocks by night,
   God with us is now residing,
   Yonder shines the Infant Light:

   Come and worship . . .

3 Sages, leave your contemplations,
   Brighter visions beam afar;
   Seek the great Desire of Nations,
   Ye have seen his natal star:

   Come and worship . . .

4 Saints before the altar bending
   Watching long in hope and fear,
   Suddenly the Lord, descending,
   In his temple shall appear:

   Come and worship . . .

5 Though an infant now we view him,
   He shall fill his Father's throne,
   Gather all the nations to him;
   Every knee shall then bow down:

   Come and worship . . .

Angels, shepherds, wise men and saints are summoned in turn to come and worship the new-born King. The final verse comes originally from another carol, in The Christmas Box *(1825). 'Come and worship' are Montgomery's own words for the refrain, rather than 'Gloria in excelsis Deo', which belonged to no. 58, the old French carol which he was translating.*

The harmony for 'Iris' is by Martin Shaw (1875–1958), adapted by the editors.

James Montgomery (1771–1854) and Anon.

58 *Les anges dans nos campagnes*

1 Les anges dans nos campagnes
   Ont entonné l'hymne des cieux;
   Et l'écho de nos montagnes
   Redit ce chant mélodieux:

   Gloria in excelsis Deo!
   Gloria in excelsis Deo!

2 Bergers, pour qui cette fête?
   Quel est l'objet de tous ces chants?
   Quel vainqueur, quelle conquête
   Mérite ces cris triomphants?

   Gloria in excelsis Deo! . . .

3 Ils annoncent la naissance
   Du libérateur d'Israël,
   Et pleins de reconnaissance
   Chantent en ce jour solennel.

   Gloria in excelsis Deo! . . .

French, 18th century
The original of nos 5 and 90.

90 *Shepherds in the field abiding*

1 Shepherds in the field abiding,
   Tell us, when the seraph bright
   Greeted you with wondrous tiding,
   What you saw and heard that night.

   Gloria in excelsis Deo!
   Gloria in excelsis Deo!

2 We beheld — it is no fable —
   God incarnate, King of Bliss,
   Swathed and cradled in a stable,
   And the angel strain was this:

   Gloria in excelsis Deo! . . .

3 Choristers on high were singing
   Jesus and his virgin birth,
   Heavenly bells the while a-ringing
   'Peace, good-will to men on earth'.

   Gloria in excelsis Deo! . . .

Tr. George Ratcliffe Woodward (1848–1934)
This version is sung in Canada.

6 *As Joseph was a-walking, he heard an angel sing*
(Cherry Tree Carol) Joseph

1 As Joseph was a-walking, he heard an angel sing,
   This night shall be born our heavenly King.
   He neither shall be born in housen nor in hall,
   Nor in the place of Paradise, but in an ox's stall.
   Noel, Noel.

2 As Joseph was a-walking, he heard an angel sing,
   This night shall be born our heavenly King.
   He neither shall be clothèd in purple nor in pall,
   But all in fair linen as wear babies all.
   Noel, Noel.

3 As Joseph was a-walking, he heard an angel sing,
   This night shall be born our heavenly King.
   He neither shall be rockèd in silver nor in gold,
   But in a wooden cradle that rocks on the mould.
   Noel, Noel.

4 As Joseph was a-walking, he heard an angel sing,
   This night shall be born our heavenly King.
   He neither shall be christenèd in white wine nor in red,
   But in the fair spring water, as we were christenèd.
   Noel, Noel.

Part 2 of 'The Cherry Tree Carol', once one of the most popular of all folk carols, and traditionally sung on Christmas Eve. (Part 1 is the legend of Joseph and Mary talking in a cherry orchard, which also appears in the Coventry Mysteries.)

'Joseph' is by R. R. Terry (1865–1938), organist at Westminster Cathedral, who became very interested in folk song revival.

English traditional

7 *As with gladness men of old* Dix

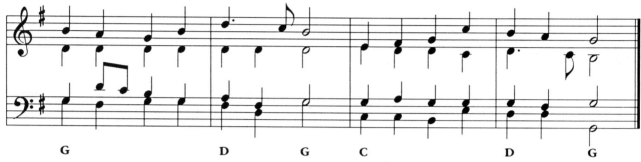

1. As with gladness men of old
   Did the guiding star behold,
   As with joy they hailed its light,
   Leading onward, beaming bright,
   So, most gracious God, may we
   Evermore be led to thee.

2. As with joyful steps they sped
   To that lowly manger-bed,
   There to bend the knee before
   Him whom heaven and earth adore,
   So may we with willing feet
   Ever seek thy mercy-seat.

3. As they offered gifts most rare
   At that manger rude and bare,
   So may we with holy joy,
   Pure, and free from sin's alloy,
   All our costliest treasures bring,
   Christ, to thee our heavenly King.

4. Holy Jesu, every day
   Keep us in the narrow way;
   And, when earthly things are past,
   Bring our ransomed souls at last
   Where they need no star to guide,
   Where no clouds thy glory hide.

5. In the heavenly country bright
   Need they no created light;
   Thou its Light, its Joy, its Crown,
   Thou its Sun which goes not down:
   There for ever may we sing
   Alleluyas to our King.

Dix was a businessman who wrote the hymn in 1860, while recovering from a serious illness. The first three verses compare the journey of the three wise men (Matthew 2.1–11) to our own spiritual pilgrimage, and the hymn ends with prayer and worship.

'Dix' is abridged by W. H. Monk (1823–89) from a chorale by Conrad Kocher (1786–1872).

W. Chatterton Dix (1837–98)

8 *A virgin most pure, as the prophet do tell* English traditional melody

1 A virgin most pure, as the prophet do tell,
  Hath brought forth a baby as it hath befel,
  To be our Redeemer from death, hell, and sin,
  Which Adam's transgression had wrappèd us in.

   Aye, and therefore be merry;
   Rejoice, and be you merry;
   Set sorrow aside;
   Christ Jesus our Saviour was born on this tide.

2 At Bethlem in Jewry a city there was,
  Where Joseph and Mary together did pass,
  And there to be taxèd with many one moe,
  For Caesar commanded the same should be so.

   Aye, and therefore be merry; . . .

3 But when they had entered the city so fair,
  A number of people so mighty was there,
  That Joseph and Mary, whose substance was small,
  Could find in the inn there no lodging at all.

   Aye, and therefore be merry; . . .

4 Then were they constrained in a stable to lie,
  Where horses and asses they used for to tie;
  Their lodging so simple they took it no scorn;
  But against the next morning our Saviour was born.

   Aye, and therefore be merry; . . .

5 The King of all kings to this world being brought,
  Small store of fine linen to wrap him was sought;
  But when she had swaddled her young son so sweet,
  Within an ox manger she laid him to sleep.

   Aye, and therefore be merry; . . .

6 Then God sent an angel from Heaven so high,
  To certain poor shepherds in fields where they lie,
  And bade them no longer in sorrow to stay,
  Because that our Saviour was born on this day.

   Aye, and therefore be merry; . . .

7 Then presently after the shepherds did spy
  A number of angels that stood in the sky;
  They joyfully talkèd and sweetly did sing,
  To God be all glory, our heavenly King.

   Aye, and therefore be merry; . . .

This traditional carol, first printed in 1834, follows St Luke's Nativity story.

The tune needs to be kept flowing: think of one beat in a bar.

English traditional

9 *Away in a manger, no crib for a bed* Cradle Song

1. Away in a manger, no crib for a bed,
   The little Lord Jesus laid down his sweet head.
   The stars in the bright sky looked down where he lay,
   The little Lord Jesus asleep on the hay.

2. The cattle are lowing, the baby awakes,
   But little Lord Jesus no crying he makes.
   I love thee, Lord Jesus! Look down from the sky,
   And stay by my side until morning is nigh.

3. Be near me, Lord Jesus; I ask thee to stay
   Close by me forever, and love me, I pray.
   Bless all the dear children in thy tender care,
   And fit us for heaven, to live with thee there.

'Away in a manger' first appeared anonymously in America in 1885. Both words and tune have in the past been mistakenly ascribed to Martin Luther. Verse 3 was added by J. T. McFarland about 1906. It is rather sentimental, but it hits the spot for most of us at Christmas.

'Cradle Song' was written for these words by the gospel song-writer W. J. Kirkpatrick (1838–1921). It should be sung smoothly, but not too slowly, if possible singing each line in one breath.

Lutheran

---

10 *Bethlehem, of noble cities* Stuttgart

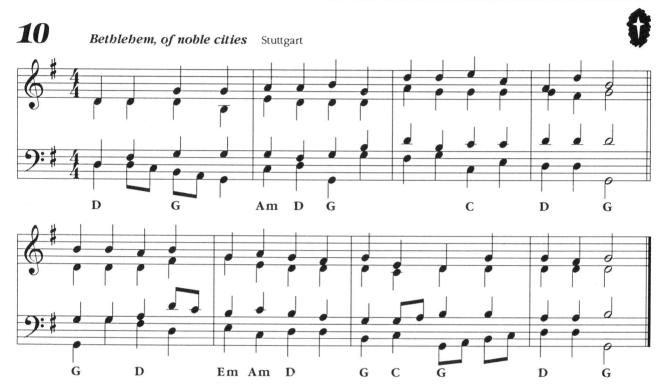

1. Bethlehem, of noble cities
   None can once with thee compare;
   Thou alone the Lord from heaven
   Didst for us incarnate bear.

2. Fairer than the sun at morning
   Was the star that told his birth;
   To the lands their God announcing,
   Seen in fleshly form on earth.

3. By its lambent beauty guided
   See the eastern kings appear;
   See them bend, their gifts to offer,
   Gifts of incense, gold and myrrh.

4. Solemn things of mystic meaning:
   Incense doth the God disclose,
   Gold a royal child proclaimeth,
   Myrrh a future tomb foreshows.

5. Holy Jesu, in thy brightness
   To the Gentile world displayed,
   With the Father and the Spirit
   Endless praise to thee be paid.

One of very few ancient hymns to have been handed down from the early Church's celebration of the Epiphany. It reflects the teaching of the early Fathers about the symbolic meaning of the three gifts.

Another version, beginning 'Earth hath many a noble city', is also sung to 'Stuttgart', a majestic tune by C. F. Witt (1660–1716).

Prudentius (348–410), tr. Edward Caswall (1814–78)

11 — *Born in the night, Mary's Child*

1. Born in the night, Mary's Child,
   A long way from your home;
   Coming in need, Mary's Child,
   Born in a borrowed room:

2. Clear shining light, Mary's Child,
   Your face lights up our way:
   Light of the world, Mary's Child,
   Dawn on our darkened day.

3. Truth of our life, Mary's Child,
   You tell us God is good:
   Prove it is true, Mary's Child,
   Go to your cross of wood.

4. Hope of the world, Mary's Child,
   You're coming soon to reign:
   King of the earth, Mary's Child,
   Walk in our streets again.

Like 'Ballad of the Homeless Christ' (no. 2), a carol inspired by the social issues faced during Geoffrey Ainger's 1960s Notting Hill ministry.

Geoffrey Ainger (b. 1925)

Words and music © Geoffrey Ainger.
Used by permission of Stainer and Bell.
USA © 1964, Galliard Ltd. Used by permission of Galaxy Music Corp., Boston.

12 — *Brightest and best of the sons of the morning*   Epiphany

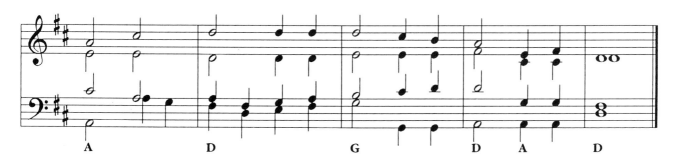

1 Brightest and best of the sons of the morning,
Dawn on our darkness and lend us thine aid;
Star of the East, the horizon adorning,
Guide where our infant Redeemer is laid.

2 Cold on his cradle the dew-drops are shining,
Low lies his head with the beasts of the stall:
Angels adore him in slumber reclining,
Maker and Monarch and Saviour of all.

3 Say, shall we yield him, in costly devotion,
Odours of Edom and offerings divine?
Gems of the mountain and pearls of the ocean,
Myrrh from the forest or gold from the mine?

4 Vainly we offer each ample oblation,
Vainly with gifts would his favour secure;
Richer by far is the heart's adoration,
Dearer to God are the prayers of the poor.

5 Brightest and best of the sons of the morning,
Dawn on our darkness and lend us thine aid;
Star of the East, the horizon adorning,
Guide where our infant Redeemer is laid.

Poetic nature imagery is used to paint the Nativity scene in this hymn, first published in 1811. The purpose is to make us imagine the scene and then think deeply about what God really wants from us.

'Epiphany', by F. J. Thrupp (1827–67), is the most cheerful of the tunes to which the words are commonly sung.

Reginald Heber (1783–1826)

13 Child in the manger Bunessan

1 Child in the manger,
Infant of Mary,
Outcast and stranger,
Lord of all!
Child who inherits
All our transgressions,
All our demerits
On him fall.

2 Once the most holy
Child of Salvation,
Gentle and lowly,
Lived below;
Now, as our glorious
Mighty Redeemer,
See him victorious
O'er each foe.

3 Prophets foretold him,
Infant of Wonder;
Angels behold him
On his throne;
Worthy our Saviour
Of all their praises;
Happy for ever

The Gaelic melody 'Bunessan' has become popularly associated with the words of 'Morning has broken', and once reached the hit parade Top Ten; but it belongs originally to this carol.

Lachlan Macbean (1853–1931), after Mary MacDonald (1789–1872)

14 *Child of Mary, newly born* — Lynch's Lullaby

1. Child of Mary, newly born,
   Softly in a manger laid,
   Wake to wonder on this morn,
   View the world your fingers made.
   Starlight shone above your bed,
   Lantern-light about your birth:
   Morning sunlight crown your head,
   Light and Life of all the earth!

2. Child of Mary, grown and strong,
   Traveller, teacher, young and free,
   See him stride the hills along,
   Christ the Man of Galilee.
   Wisdom from a world above
   Now by waiting hearts is heard:
   Hear him speak the words of love,
   Christ the true eternal Word.

3 Child of Mary, grief and loss,
  All the sum of human woe,
  Crown of thorn and cruel cross,
  Mark the path you choose to go.
  Man of Sorrows, born to save,
  Bearing all our sins and pains:
  From his cross and empty grave
  Christ the Lord of Glory reigns.

4 Child of Mary, gift of grace,
  By whose birth shall all be well,
  One with us in form and face,
  God with us, Emmanuel!
  Night is past and shadows fled,
  Wake to joy on Christmas morn:
  Sunlight crown the Saviour's head,
  Christ the Prince of Peace is born.

*It is Christ the young hero sent from heaven —
almost closer to the demigod of Greek mythology than Isaiah's
vision of the suffering servant — whose birth is joyfully
celebrated in Bishop Dudley-Smith's attractive carol.*

*'Lynch's Lullaby', arranged by Donald Davison from a
tune in J.P. Lynch's* Melodies of Ireland *(c. 1845), is of
appealing simplicity, and should be sung calmly.*

Timothy Dudley-Smith (b. 1926)

Words © Timothy Dudley-Smith. Used by permission.

Music © Oxford University Press. Used by permission.

15 *Christians awake! Salute the happy morn* Yorkshire

1 Christians awake! salute the happy morn
  Whereon the Saviour of the world was born;
  Rise to adore the mystery of love
  Which hosts of angels chanted from above;
  With them the joyful tidings first begun
  Of God incarnate and the Virgin's son.

2 Then to the watchful shepherds it was told,
  Who heard the angelic herald's voice, 'Behold,
  I bring good tidings of a Saviour's birth
  To you and all the nations upon earth:
  This day hath God fulfilled his promised word,
  This day is born a Saviour, Christ the Lord.'

3 He spake; and straightway that celestial choir
  In hymns of joy, unknown before, conspire;
  The praises of redeeming love they sing,
  And heaven's whole orb with alleluyas ring:
  God's highest glory was their anthem still,
  Peace on the earth, and mutual goodwill.

4 To Bethl'em straight th'enlightened shepherds run
  To see the wonder that the Lord has done,
  And find, with Joseph and the blessèd Maid,
  Her Son, the Saviour, in a manger laid;
  Then to their flocks, still praising God, return,
  And their glad hearts with holy rapture burn.

5 O may we keep and ponder in our mind
  God's wondrous love in saving humankind;
  Trace we the Babe, who hath retrieved our loss,
  From his poor manger to his bitter cross;
  Tread in his steps, assisted by his grace,
  Till our first heavenly state again takes place.

6 Then may we hope, th'angelic hosts among,
  To sing, redeemed, a glad triumphal song.
  He that was born upon this joyful day
  Around us all his glory shall display;
  Saved by his love, incessant we shall sing
  Eternal praise to heav'n's almighty King.

Byrom's little daughter, Dolly, asked him to write her a poem as a Christmas present. On Christmas morning 1749 she found on her plate these lines on a sheet of paper headed 'Christmas Day. For Dolly.' The following Christmas the Byroms were woken up by the choir of Stockport parish church singing 'Christians awake!' beneath their windows, to the tune 'Yorkshire' that John Wainwright (1723–68), their local church organist, had especially composed for it.

John Byrom (1692–1763)

16 Come, come, come to the manger — English traditional melody

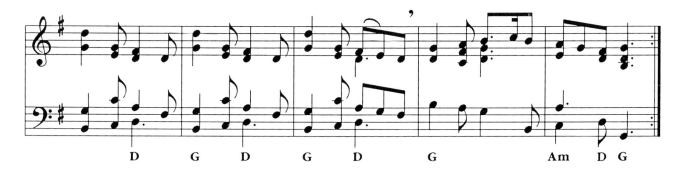

Come, come, come to the manger,
Children, come to the children's King;
Sing, sing, chorus of angels,
Stars of morning, o'er Bethlehem sing!

1 He lies 'mid the beasts of the stall,
Who is Maker and Lord of us all;
The wintry wind blows cold and dreary,
See, he weeps, the world is weary,
Lord, have pity and mercy on me.

  Come, come, come to the manger, . . .

2 To the manger of Bethlehem come,
To the Saviour Emmanuel's home;
The heavenly hosts above are singing,
Set the Christmas bells a-ringing,
Lord, have pity and mercy on me.

  Come, come, come to the manger, . . .

A 'wintry wind' blows through this children's carol, which returns, nevertheless, to a joyful refrain.
The lively traditional tune lends itself to simple accompaniment on recorders or percussion.

John Robert, Abbot of Downside

Words © John Robert. Used by kind permission.

17 *Come, they told me (The Little Drummer)* Czech carol melody

1 Come, they told me, parum pum pum pum,
   A new-born king to see, parum pum pum pum,
   Our finest gifts we bring, parum pum pum pum,
   To lay before the king, parum pum pum pum,
   Rum pum pum pum, rum pum pum pum.
   So to honour him, parum pum pum pum,
   When we come.

2 Baby Jesus, parum pum pum pum,
   I am a poor child too, parum pum pum pum,
   I have no gift to bring, parum pum pum pum,
   That's fit to give our king, parum pum pum pum,
   Rum pum pum pum, rum pum pum pum.
   Shall I play for you, parum pum pum pum,
   On my drum?

3 Mary nodded, parum pum pum pum,
   The ox and ass kept time, parum pum pum pum,
   I played my drum for him, parum pum pum pum,
   I played my best for him, parum pum pum pum,
   Rum pum pum pum, rum pum pum pum.
   Then he smiled at me, parum pum pum pum,
   Me and my drum.

The Christmas story seen through the eyes of a poor child, who visits the manger and, having no other gift, plays the drum for Jesus and Mary. It has been recorded by many famous names in the pop music world.
   The tune is a traditional Czech carol melody.

Katherine K. Davis, Harry Simeone and Henry Onorati

Words and music © 1958 Mills Music Inc., USA, and International Music Corp., USA; Chappell Music Ltd, London W1Y 3FA

---

18 *Come, thou long-expected Jesus*   Cross of Jesus

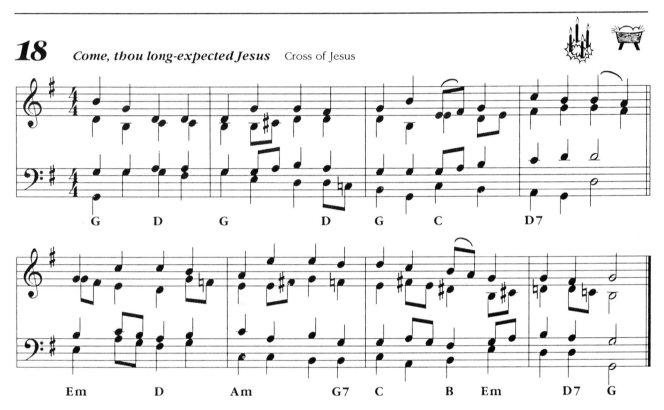

1 Come, thou long-expected Jesus,
   Born to set thy people free,
   From our fears and sins release us,
   Let us find our rest in thee.

2 Israel's strength and consolation,
   Hope of all the earth thou art,
   Dear desire of every nation,
   Joy of every longing heart.

3 Born thy people to deliver,
   Born a child and yet a king,
   Born to reign in us for ever,
   Now thy gracious kingdom bring.

4 By thine own eternal spirit,
   Rule in all our hearts alone;
   By thine all-sufficient merit
   Raise us to thy glorious throne.

A hymn that emphasizes the kingship of Jesus, this first appeared in Charles Wesley's Hymns for the Nativity of our Lord *(1744) in two eight-line verses.*
   It is now usually sung, as here, to the fine four-line tune 'Cross of Jesus', by John Stainer (1840–1901).

Charles Wesley (1707–88)

19 Dans cette étable

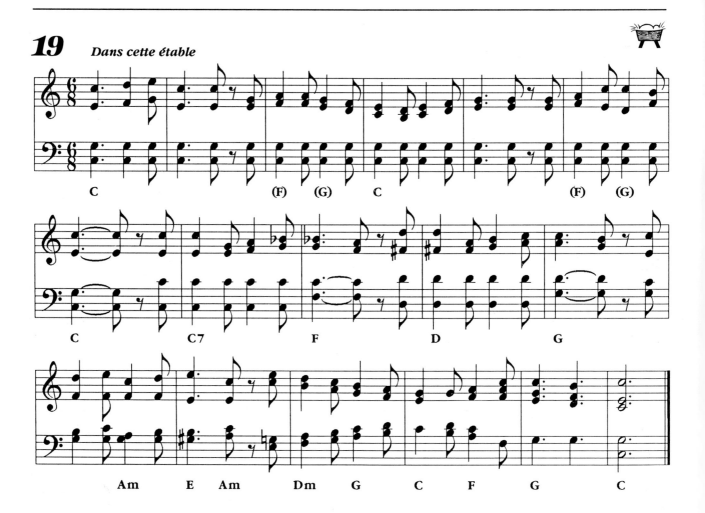

1 Dans cette étable
   Que Jésus est charmant,
   Qu'il est aimable
   Dans son abaissement!
   Que d'attraits à la fois!
   Tous les palais des rois
   N'ont rien de comparable
   Aux beautés que je vois dans cette étable!

2 Plus de misère!
   Un Dieu souffre pour nous,
   Et de son Père
   Désarme le courroux;
   C'est en notre faveur
   Qu'il est dans la douleur.
   Pouvait-il pour nous plaire
   Unir à sa grandeur plus de misère?

3 Que sa puissance
   Reluit bien en ce jour!
   Malgré l'enfance
   Où le reduit l'amour.
   Notre ennemi dompté,
   L'enfer déconcerté,
   Font voir qu'à sa naissance
   Rien n'est plus redouté que sa puissance!

No translation is quite satisfactory or necessary for this simply worded traditional French carol. It expresses the appeal of Jesus' humble birth in a poor stable, in contrast with the empty trappings of earthly power, and compares the love and sweetness of the child, born into poverty and suffering, to the acts of love and suffering that he will later endure in his life and death.

It is sometimes called 'Gounod's Bethlehem' because the traditional tune was arranged by Charles Gounod (1818–93).

Fléchier (1632–1710)

20 *Deck the hall with boughs of holly*   Nos Galan

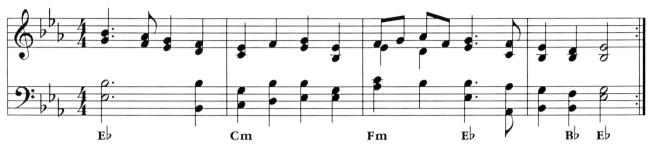

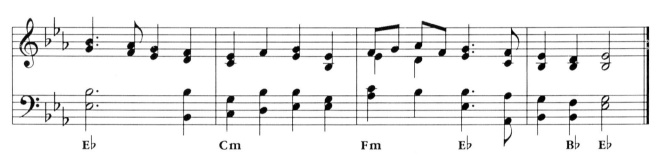

1. Deck the hall with boughs of holly,
   Fa la la la la, la la la la.
   'Tis the season to be jolly,
   Fa la la la la, la la la la.
   Don we now our gay apparel,
   Fa la la, la la la, la la la.
   Troll the ancient Yuletide carol,
   Fa la la la la, la la la la.

2. See the blazing Yule before us,
   Fa la la la la, la la la la.
   Strike the harp and join the chorus,
   Fa la la la la, la la la la.
   Follow me in merry measure,
   Fa la la, la la la, la la la.
   While I tell of Yuletide treasure,
   Fa la la la la, la la la la.

3. Fast away the old year passes,
   Fa la la la la, la la la la.
   Hail the new, ye lads and lasses,
   Fa la la la la, la la la la.
   Sing we joyous all together,
   Fa la la la la, la la la la.
   Heedless of the wind and weather,
   Fa la la la la, la la la la.

A secular carol, long popular with carol singers out on cold winter nights. Also suitable for New Year services.

'Nos Galan' is a traditional Welsh tune, arranged here by John Barnard.

Welsh traditional

Arrangement © John Barnard/Jubilate Hymns. Used by permission.

21 *Deep peace of the running wave to you (A Gaelic Blessing)*

Deep peace of the running wave to you,
Deep peace of the flowing air to you,
Deep peace of the quiet earth to you,
Deep peace of the shining stars to you,
Deep peace of the gentle night to you,
Moon and stars pour their healing light on you,
Deep peace of Christ,
Of Christ the light of the world to you,
Deep peace of Christ to you.

John Rutter's setting of an ancient Gaelic blessing, which was commissioned by a Methodist church in the USA for Mel Olson, has become popular with non-choral singers, mainly through being sung on BBC TV's Songs of Praise. John Rutter has made a simplified arrangement especially for this collection, so that all carol singers can attempt this beautiful piece, which is ideal for ending a carol service.

Ancient Gaelic blessing, adapted John Rutter (b. 1945)

Words and musical arrangement © John Rutter. Used by permission of the Royal School of Church Music.

22   *Ding-dong, ding, ding-a-dong-a-ding (Up, good Christen folk)*

Ding-dong, ding, ding-a-dong-a-ding:
Ding-dong, ding-dong, ding-a-dong-ding.

1 Up! good Christen folk, and listen
How the merry church bells ring.
And from steeple bid good people
Come adore the new-born King:

2 Tell the story how from glory
God came down at Christmas-tide,
Bringing gladness, chasing sadness,
Show'ring blessings far and wide.

3 Born of mother, blest o'er other,
Ex Maria Virgine,
In a stable ('tis no fable),
Christus natus hodie.

Ding-dong, ding, ding-a-dong-a-ding:
Ding-dong, ding-dong, ding-a-dong-ding.

As in 'Ding dong! merrily on high' (no. 23), Woodward wants carol singers to imitate the sound of the Christmas church bells.
The melody is from Piae Cantiones *(1582).*

George Ratcliffe Woodward (1848–1934)

23 Ding dong! merrily on high Branle de l'officiale

1 Ding dong! merrily on high
In heav'n the bells are ringing:
Ding dong! verily the sky
Is riv'n with angel-singing.

  Gloria! Hosanna in excelsis!
  Gloria! Hosanna in excelsis!

2 E'en so here below, below,
Let steeple bells be swungen,
And i-o, i-o, i-o,
By priest and people sungen.

  Gloria! Hosanna in excelsis! . . .

3 Pray you, dutifully prime
Your matin chime, ye ringers;
May you beautifully rime
Your evetime song, ye singers.

  Gloria! Hosanna in excelsis! . . .

A carol, to a 16th-century French tune, that imitates and praises the sound of Christmas church bells. It needs plenty of bounce in performance.
'I-o' should be pronounced 'ee-o'.

George Ratcliffe Woodward (1848–1934)

24 Every star shall sing a carol

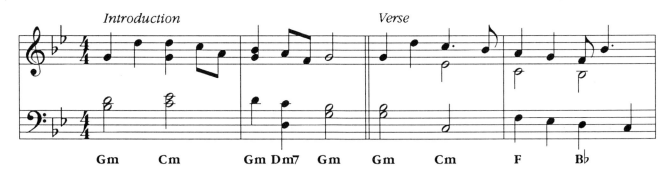

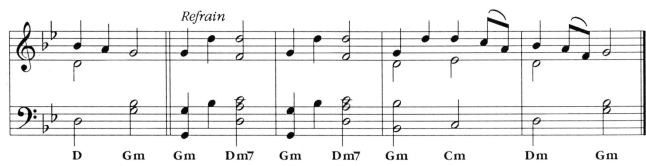

1 Every star shall sing a carol;
  Every creature, high or low,
  Come and praise the King of Heaven
  By whatever name you know.

  God above, Man below,
  Holy is the name I know.

2 When the King of all creation
  Had a cradle on the earth,
  Holy was the human body,
  Holy was the human birth.

  God above, Man below, . . .

3 Who can tell what other cradle
  High above the Milky Way
  Still may rock the King of Heaven
  On another Christmas Day?

  God above, Man below, . . .

4 Who can count how many crosses
  Still to come or long ago
  Crucify the King of Heaven?
  Holy is the name I know.

  God above, Man below, . . .

5 Who can tell what other body
  He will hallow for his own?
  I will praise the Son of Mary,
  Brother of my blood and bone.

  God above, Man below, . . .

6 Every star and every planet,
  Every creature high and low,
  Come and praise the King of Heaven
  By whatever name you know.

  God above, Man below, . . .

'By whatever name you know.' Anyone with a sense of the numinous, but lacking in certainty or desire to possess a fixed set of truths, will like Sydney Carter's words, born out of doubt, bright with hope. He says 'Song, God, a waving possibility: you must trust it, travel with it — or it is not there'.

Sydney Carter (b. 1915)

Words and music © Sydney Carter. Used by permission of Stainer & Bell.
USA © 1961, Galliard Ltd. Used by permission of Galaxy Music Corp., Boston.

25 *Girls and boys, leave your toys, make no noise*
(Zither Carol) Czech folk dance

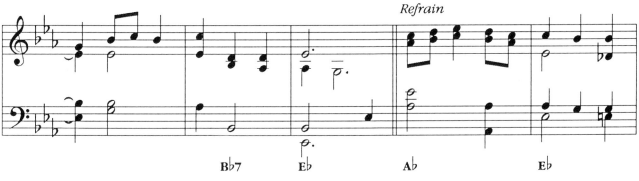

1 Girls and boys, leave your toys, make no noise,
  Kneel at his crib and worship him.
  At thy shrine, Child divine, we are thine,
  Our Saviour's here.

   'Hallelujah' the church bells ring,
   'Hallelujah' the angels sing,
   'Hallelujah' from everything.
   All must draw near.

2 On that day, far away, Jesus lay,
  Angels were watching round his head.
  Holy child, mother mild, undefiled,
  We sing thy praise.

   'Hallelujah' the church bells ring, . . .

3 Shepherds came at the fame of thy name,
  Angels their guide to Bethlehem.
  In that place, saw thy face filled with grace,
  Stood at thy door.

   'Hallelujah' the church bells ring, . . .

Words by Sir Malcolm Sargent, who helped so many to enjoy music and to love singing. Children are called to leave their toys and games, and come and worship at the manger with the shepherds and angels.
  Always known as the 'Zither Carol'; the tune is a traditional Czech folk dance.

Malcolm Sargent (1895–1967)

Words and music used by permission of Oxford University Press.

26 *Gloria, gloria, in excelsis Deo* Gloria

Gloria, gloria, in excelsis Deo,
Gloria, gloria, alleluia!
Et in terra pax hominibus
Bonae voluntatis.

A canon from Taizé, an ecumenical Christian community in Burgundy, France, which today attracts huge numbers of pilgrims, particularly young people, from all around the world. This 'Gloria' has become very popular with the pilgrims, and is sung, as part of the Christmas liturgy, in four-part canon.

Jacques Berthier

Words and music © Ateliers et Presses de Taizé, 71250 Taizé Communauté, France. Used by permission.

27. God rest ye merry, gentlemen — London Carol Melody

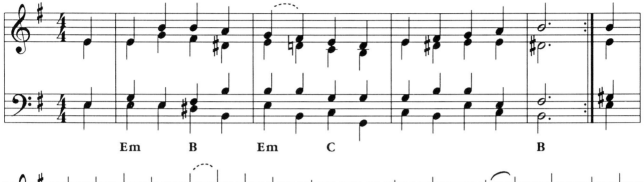

1. God rest ye merry, gentlemen,
   Let nothing you dismay,
   Remember Christ our Saviour
   Was born on Christmas Day,
   To save us all from Satan's power
   When we were gone astray:

   O tidings of comfort and joy,
   Comfort and joy!
   O tidings of comfort and joy!

2. From God our heavenly Father
   A blessèd angel came,
   And unto certain shepherds
   Brought tidings of the same,
   How that in Bethlehem was born
   The son of God by name:

   O tidings of comfort and joy, . . .

3. And when they came to Bethlehem
   Where our dear Saviour lay,
   They found him in a manger,
   Where oxen feed on hay;
   His mother Mary kneeling down,
   Unto the Lord did pray:

   O tidings of comfort and joy, . . .

4. Now to the Lord sing praises,
   All you within this place,
   And with true love and fellowship
   Each other now embrace;
   This holy tide of Christmas
   All other doth efface:

   O tidings of comfort and joy, . . .

A popular traditional carol, harmonized by John Stainer (1840–1901). Frequently heard on the streets of London in the 18th and 19th centuries, this version of St Luke's Christmas story has the purpose of drawing everyone (not only gentlemen!) into the experience of the shepherds. The first four words are, of course, a greeting, so the placing of the comma is important.

English traditional

28. Good King Wenceslas looked out — Tempus Adest Floridum

1. Good King Wenceslas looked out
   On the Feast of Stephen,
   When the snow lay round about,
   Deep, and crisp, and even:
   Brightly shone the moon that night,
   Though the frost was cruel,
   When a poor man came in sight
   Gath'ring winter fuel.

2. 'Hither, page, and stand by me,
   If thou know'st it, telling.
   Yonder peasant, who is he?
   Where and what his dwelling?'
   'Sire, he lives a good league hence,
   Underneath the mountain,
   Right against the forest fence,
   By Saint Agnes' fountain.'

3. 'Bring me flesh, and bring me wine,
   Bring me pine logs hither:
   Thou and I will see him dine,
   When we bear them thither.'
   Page and monarch, forth they went,
   Forth they went together;
   Through the rude wind's wild lament
   And the bitter weather.

4. 'Sire, the night is darker now,
   And the wind blows stronger;
   Fails my heart, I know not how;
   I can go no longer.'
   'Mark my footsteps, good my page;
   Tread thou in them boldly:
   Thou shalt find the winter's rage
   Freeze thy blood less coldly.'

5. In his master's steps he trod,
   Where the snow lay dinted;
   Heat was in the very sod
   Which the Saint had printed.
   Therefore, Christians all, be sure,
   Wealth or rank possessing,
   Ye who now will bless the poor,
   Shall yourselves find blessing.

A carol that tells an imaginary story based on a real person. The Feast of Stephen is the day after Christmas, i.e. Boxing Day; Wenceslas (c. 907–929), prince and martyr, became the patron saint of Bohemia and the symbol of Czech independence.

John Mason Neale (1818–66)

29 Go, tell it on the mountain

Go, tell it on the mountain,
Over the hills and everywhere;
Go, tell it on the mountain
That Jesus Christ is born!

1 While shepherds sat a-watching
Their silent flocks by night,
There shone throughout the heavens
A great and glorious light.

　Go, tell it on the mountain, . . .

2 The shepherds feared and trembled
When, high above the earth,
Rang out the angel chorus
That hailed our Saviour's birth.

　Go, tell it on the mountain, . . .

American traditional

30 Hail, Mary, full of grace — Ave Maria

1. Hail, Mary, full of grace,
   You are blessed, the Lord is with you.
   Through his angel God is asking
   You to be the mother of his son.
   Speak, Mary, for us all:
   There's no sweeter music heard
   Than your gladly whispered answer
   'Let it be to me according to your word.'

2. Good news for humankind;
   Joseph hears the joyful message:
   God will come to us in Jesus,
   'He will save his people from their sins'.
   Jesus, Emmanuel,
   May my wayward will be stirred
   Day by day to pray with Mary:
   'Let it be to me according to your word.'

A new carol with a 'gladly whispered' prayer in each verse. It remembers that Joseph, too, shared in the extraordinary experience of being visited by angels.

Patrick Appleford (b. 1925)

Words and music © Patrick Appleford 1990. Used by kind permission.

31 Hail to the Lord's Anointed!   Crüger

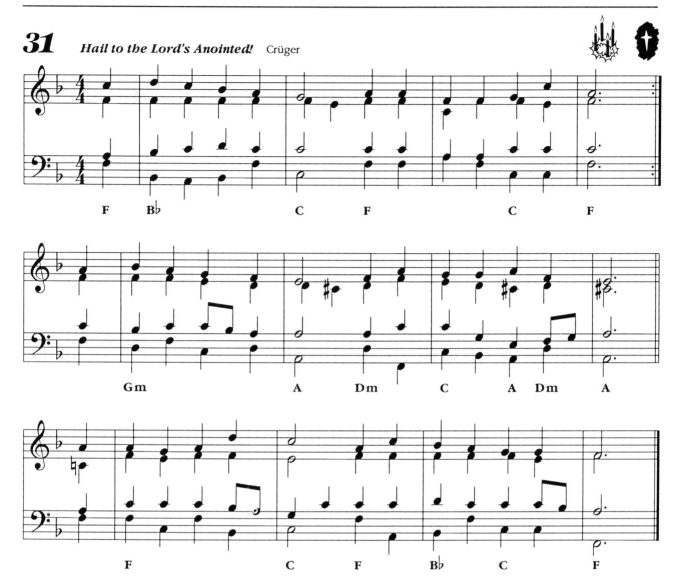

1 Hail to the Lord's Anointed!
Great David's greater Son;
Hail, in the time appointed,
His reign on earth begun!
He comes to break oppression,
To set the captive free;
To take away transgression,
And rule in equity.

2 He comes with succour speedy
To those who suffer wrong;
To help the poor and needy,
And bid the weak be strong;
To give them songs for sighing,
Their darkness turn to light,
Whose souls, condemned and dying,
Were precious in his sight.

3 He shall come down like showers
Upon the fruitful earth,
And love, joy, hope, like flowers,
Spring in his path to birth:
Before him on the mountains
Shall peace the herald go;
And righteousness in fountains
From hill to valley flow.

4 Kings shall fall down before him,
And gold and incense bring;
All nations shall adore him,
His praise all people sing;
To him shall prayer unceasing
And daily vows ascend;
His kingdom still increasing,
A kingdom without end.

5 O'er every foe victorious,
He on his throne shall rest,
From age to age more glorious,
All-blessing and all-blest:
The tide of time shall never
His covenant remove;
His name shall stand for ever;
That name to us is Love.

A free paraphrase of Psalm 72, and a strong, missionary hymn, by one of the foremost social reformers of his day.
  'Crüger' is an adaptation by W. H. Monk (1823–89), in 1861, of a 17th-century chorale by Johann Crüger (1598–1662). It needs to be sung with passion and dignity.

James Montgomery (1771–1854)

32   *Hark! A herald voice is calling*   Merton

1. Hark! a herald voice is calling:
   'Christ is nigh', it seems to say;
   'Cast away the dreams of darkness,
   O ye children of the day!'

2. Startled at the solemn warning,
   Let the earth-bound soul arise;
   Christ, her Sun, all sloth dispelling,
   Shines upon the morning skies.

3. Lo! the Lamb, so long expected,
   Comes with pardon down from Heaven;
   Let us haste, with tears of sorrow,
   One and all to be forgiven;

4. So when next he comes in glory,
   And earth's final hour draws near,
   May he then as our defender
   On the clouds of heaven appear.

5. Honour, glory, virtue, merit,
   To the Father and the Son,
   With the co-eternal Spirit,
   While unending ages run.

Based on Romans 13.11 and Luke 21.25–27, this was the Lauds hymn during Advent in the Sarum and other ancient prayer books. The words have been extensively altered by different editors over the years, and we hope this version brings out the truth for people of today.
   The tune, 'Merton', is by W. H. Monk (1823–89).

Latin, 6th century, tr. Edward Caswall (1814–78), amended

33   *Hark the glad sound! the Saviour comes*   Bristol

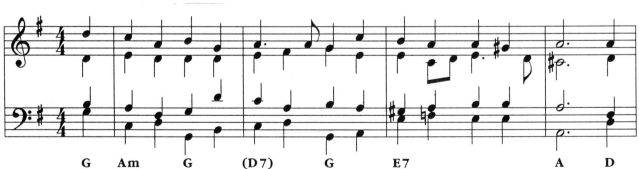

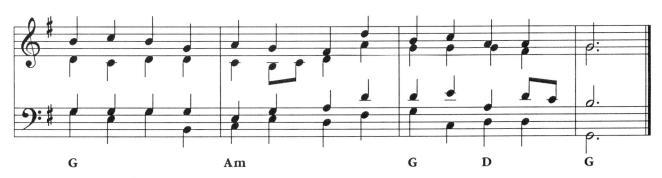

1 Hark the glad sound! the Saviour comes,
  The Saviour promised long!
  Let every heart prepare a throne,
  And every voice a song.

2 He comes the prisoners to release
  In Satan's bondage held;
  The gates of brass before him burst,
  The iron fetters yield.

3 He comes the broken heart to bind,
  The bleeding soul to cure,
  And with the treasures of his grace
  Enrich the humble poor.

4 Our glad hosannas, Prince of Peace,
  Thy welcome shall proclaim,
  And heaven's eternal arches ring
  With thy belovèd name.

The original manuscript, published in 1735, is headed 'Christ's Message, from Luke, 4.18, 19' (where Jesus read Isaiah 61.1, 2). Like many of Doddridge's hymns, this was designed to be sung immediately after he had preached on the text.
   'Bristol' comes from Ravenscroft's Psalter *(1621).*

Philip Doddridge (1702–51)

34 *Hark! the herald angels sing* Mendelssohn

1 Hark! the herald angels sing
　Glory to the new-born King;
　Peace on earth and mercy mild,
　God and sinners reconciled:
　Joyful all ye nations rise,
　Join the triumph of the skies,
　With the angelic host proclaim,
　Christ is born in Bethlehem.

　　Hark! the herald angels sing
　　Glory to the new-born King.

2 Christ, by highest heaven adored,
　Christ, the everlasting Lord,
　Late in time behold him come
　Offspring of a Virgin's womb!
　Veiled in flesh the Godhead see,
　Hail the incarnate Deity!
　Pleased as man with man to dwell,
　Jesus, our Emmanuel:

　　Hark! the herald angels sing . . .

3 Hail the heaven-born Prince of Peace!
  Hail the Sun of Righteousness!
  Light and life to all he brings,
  Risen with healing in his wings;
  Mild he lays his glory by,
  Born that man no more may die,
  Born to raise the sons of earth,
  Born to give them second birth:

    Hark! the herald angels sing . . .

Probably the best-known carol in the world. Charles Wesley's original 1743 carol ('Hark how all the welkin ring') was and is very fine in its own right, but alterations made by Whitefield and others have made it universally acclaimed.

'Mendelssohn' is an adaptation by Dr William Hayman Cummings of a chorus in Mendelssohn's secular cantata Festgesang. *The composer himself, however, considered the tune unsuitable for sacred words, describing it in a letter to his publisher as 'soldierlike and buxom'!*

The last two lines and the refrain sometimes stretch the capacity of many singers, so we have transposed the tune down; you should also notice that the last two lines of the verse have the same notes as the refrain, but a slightly different rhythm.

Charles Wesley (1707–88), G. Whitefield (in 1753), M. Madan (in 1760) and others

35 Here we go up to Bethlehem — English traditional melody

1 Here we go up to Bethlehem,
  Bethlehem, Bethlehem,
  Here we go up to Bethlehem
  On a cold and frosty morning.

2 We've got to be taxed in Bethlehem,
  Bethlehem, Bethlehem,
  We've got to be taxed in Bethlehem
  On a cold and frosty morning.

3 Where shall we stay in Bethlehem,
  Bethlehem, Bethlehem?
  Where shall we stay in Bethlehem
  On a cold and frosty morning?

New words to the traditional English melody for 'Here we go round the mulberry bush!' Written for children, and it's a good idea to ask them to make up extra verses to finish the story, which is deliberately left incomplete.

Sydney Carter (b. 1915)

Words © Sydney Carter. Used by permission of Stainer & Bell.
USA © 1965, Galliard Ltd. Used by permission of Galaxy Music Corp., Boston.

36. He smiles within his cradle
Ein Kindlein in der Wiegen

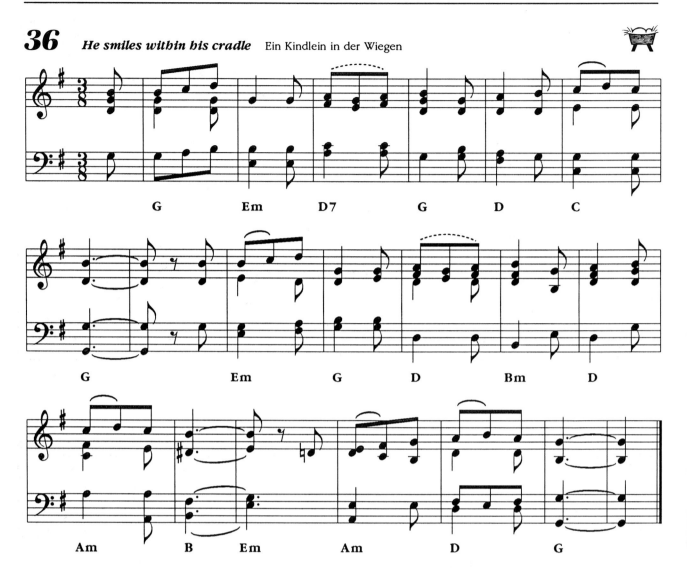

1. He smiles within his cradle,
   A babe with face so bright
   It beams most like a mirror
   Against a blaze of light:
   This babe so burning bright.

2. This babe we now declare to you
   Is Jesus Christ our Lord;
   He brings both peace and heartiness:
   Haste, haste with one accord
   To feast with Christ our Lord.

3. And who would rock the cradle
   Wherein this infant lies,
   Must rock with easy motion
   And watch with humble eyes,
   Like Mary pure and wise.

4. O Jesus, dearest babe of all
   And dearest babe of mine,
   Thy love is great, thy limbs are small.
   O, flood this heart of mine
   With overflow from thine!

Austrian, tr. Robert Graves

The Austrian words and tune 'Ein Kindlein in der Wiegen' first appeared in Vienna in 1649 in D. G. Corner's Geistliche Nachtigall. Robert Graves's 1928 translation has made this gentle lullaby carol very popular in Britain, too.

Words © Robert Graves, from the Oxford Book of Carols. Reprinted by permission of Oxford University Press. Musical arrangement © Martin Shaw. Used by permission of Oxford University Press.

37 Hills of the North, rejoice — Little Cornard

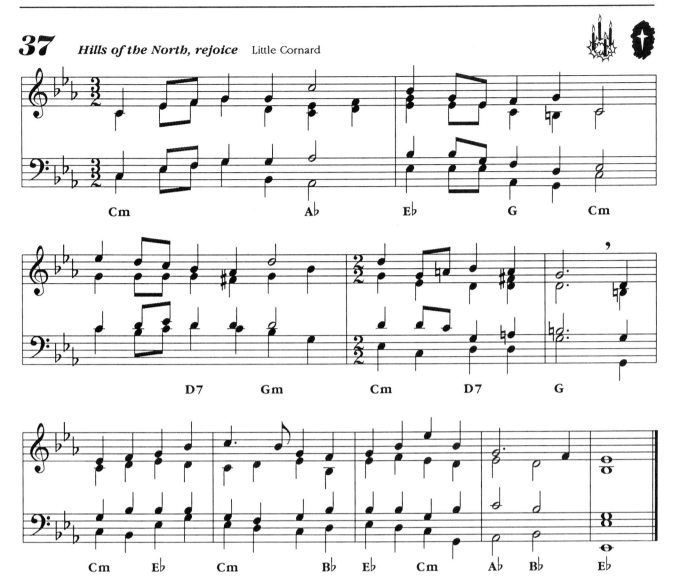

1 Hills of the North, rejoice,
  Echoing songs arise,
  Hail with united voice
  Him who made earth and skies:
  He comes in righteousness and love,
  He brings salvation from above.

2 Isles of the southern seas,
  Sing to the listening earth,
  Carry on every breeze
  Hope of a world's new birth:
  In Christ shall all be made anew,
  His word is sure, his promise true.

3 Lands of the East, arise,
  He is your brightest morn,
  Greet him with joyous eyes,
  Praise shall his path adorn:
  The God whom you have longed to know
  In Christ draws near, and calls you now.

4 Shores of the utmost West,
  Lands of the setting sun,
  Welcome the heavenly guest
  In whom the dawn has come:
  He brings a never-ending light
  Who triumphed o'er our darkest night.

5 Shout, as you journey on,
  Songs be in every mouth,
  Lo, from the North they come,
  From East and West and South:
  In Jesus all shall find their rest,
  In him shall all the earth be blest.

A stirring missionary hymn, suitable for both Advent and Epiphany. It is the one relic of a short and brilliant life, although Oakley's original words have had to be extensively revised.
  Martin Shaw (1875–1958) composed 'Little Cornard' especially for this hymn, and the change of rhythm in the last two lines adds great power.

Based on words by Charles E. Oakley (1832–65)

Words (this version) used by permission of Oxford University Press.
Music © Martin Shaw. Used by permission of William Elkin Music Services.

38 Holy Child, how still you lie — Holy Child

1 Holy Child, how still you lie!
  Safe the manger, soft the hay;
  Faint upon the eastern sky
  Breaks the dawn of Christmas Day.

2 Holy Child, whose birthday brings
  Shepherds from their field and fold,
  Angel choirs and eastern kings,
  Myrrh and frankincense and gold:

3 Holy Child, what gift of grace
  From the Father freely willed!
  In your infant form we trace
  All God's promises fulfilled.

4 Holy Child, whose human years
  Span like ours delight and pain;
  One in human joys and tears,
  One in all but sin and stain:

5 Holy Child, so far from home,
  All the lost to seek and save,
  To what dreadful death you come,
  To what dark and silent grave!

6 Holy Child, before whose name
  Powers of darkness faint and fall;
  Conquered, death and sin and shame —
  Jesus Christ is Lord of all!

7 Holy Child, how still you lie!
  Safe the manger, soft the hay;
  Clear upon the eastern sky
  Breaks the dawn of Christmas Day.

Timothy Dudley-Smith (b. 1926)

*Words © Timothy Dudley-Smith. Used by permission.
Music © Michael Baughen/Jubilate Hymns. Used by permission.*

*A quiet song addressed to Jesus in the manger, meditating on the mysterious way that all the promises surrounding his birth on Christmas morning will be fulfilled.
  Michael Baughen's tune 'Holy Child' has a different melody for alternate verses.*

39. How brightly shines the Morning Star! — Wie Schön Leuchtet der Morgenstern

1. How brightly shines the Morning Star!
   The nations see and hail afar
   The Light in Judah shining.
   Thou David's son of Jacob's race,
   The Bridegroom, and the King of Grace,
   For thee our hearts are pining!
   Lowly, holy,
   Great and glorious, thou victorious
   Prince of Graces,
   Filling all the heavenly places!

2. Though circled by the hosts on high,
   He deigns to cast a pitying eye
   Upon his helpless creature;
   The whole creation's Head and Lord,
   By highest seraphim adored,
   Assumes our very nature.
   Jesu, grant us,
   Through thy merit, to inherit
   Thy salvation;
   Hear, O hear our supplication.

3. Rejoice, ye heav'ns; thou earth, reply;
   With praise, ye sinners, fill the sky,
   For this his Incarnation.
   Incarnate God, put forth thy power,
   Ride on, ride on, great Conqueror,
   Till all know thy salvation.
   Amen, Amen!
   Alleluya, Alleluya!
   Praise be given
   Evermore by earth and heaven.

The German words, and probably the tune, were composed by Nicolai in 1599, during the same terrible pestilence as 'Wake! O Wake!' (no. 108).

Much of the popularity of this hymn is due to the tune, a famous chorale, 'Wie Schön Leuchtet der Morgenstern', that was soon set on many city chimes in Germany. This arrangement is by Felix Mendelssohn (1809–47), from his oratorio Christus.

Philipp Nicolai (1556–1608), tr. William Mercer (1811–73).

40 — How lovely on the mountains are the feet of him (Our God Reigns)

1 How lovely on the mountains are the feet of him
  Who brings good news, good news,
  Proclaiming peace, announcing news of happiness:
  Our God reigns, our God reigns!

  Our God reigns, our God reigns,
  Our God reigns, our God reigns!

2 You watchmen lift your voices joyfully as one,
  Shout for your king, your king;
  See eye to eye the Lord restoring Zion:
  Your God reigns, your God reigns!

  Your God reigns, your God reigns, ...

3 Waste places of Jerusalem, break forth with joy —
  We are redeemed, redeemed;
  The Lord has saved and comforted his people:
  Your God reigns, your God reigns!

  Your God reigns, your God reigns, ...

4 Ends of the earth, see the salvation of your God —
  Jesus is Lord, is Lord!
  Before the nations he has bared his holy arm:
  Your God reigns, your God reigns!

  Your God reigns, your God reigns, ...

Based on Isaiah 52, this rapidly became popular and has been heard at great gatherings, from the crowds at the open-air Masses during Pope John Paul II's visit to Britain in 1982, to Greenbelt festivals and Spring Harvest gatherings.

Leonard E. Smith Jr

Words and music © 1974, 1978 New Jerusalem Music. Used by permission of Thankyou Music.

41 *Il est né le divin enfant* French traditional melody

Il est né le divin enfant
Jouez hautbois, résonnez musettes;
Il est né le divin enfant
Chantons tous son avènement.

1 Ah! qu'il est beau, qu'il est charmant!
  Ah! que ses grâces sont parfaites!
  Ah! qu'il est beau, qu'il est charmant!
  Qu'il est doux ce divin enfant.

  Il est né le divin enfant . . .

2 Une étable est son logement,
  Un peu de paille est sa couchette;
  Une étable est son logement
  Pour un Dieu quel abaissement!

  Il est né le divin enfant . . .

3 Partez grands rois de l'Orient,
  Venez vous unir à nos fêtes!
  Partez grands rois de l'Orient,
  Venez adorer cet enfant.

  Il est né le divin enfant . . .

This French carol involves the instruments in a canticle of praise. A musette is a kind of aristocratic bagpipe, and also a smooth and simple pastoral dance. As you sing, imagine a droning accompaniment . . .

French traditional

---

42 *I'm standing at windows, and knocking on doors (Georgie)* — Georgie

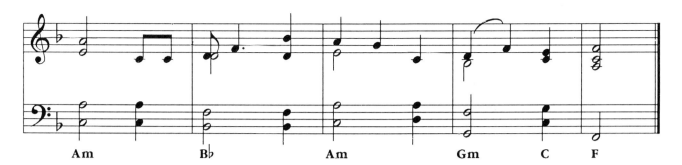

I'm standing at windows,
And knocking on doors,
I'm not sure of my welcome,
I'm too tattered and torn,
When shoppers walk round me,
I smile and I say,
'Give a penny to Georgie for Christmas Day.'
For Christmas Day, for Christmas Day,
Give a penny to Georgie for Christmas Day.

This was first performed in 1984, at the Inner London Education Authority's annual Festival of Carols: the author of both words and music was at the time a pupil at the Grey Coat Hospital School. Like 'The Little Drummer', Georgie is poor, but he is stuck in the streets of a modern city surrounded by uncaring shoppers.

It might be best to sing this through twice: each time, repeat the last two lines, but humming instead of singing the words.

Sarah Mason

Words and music © Sarah Mason. Used by kind permission.

43 In a byre near Bethlehem
(The Word of Life) Wild Mountain Thyme

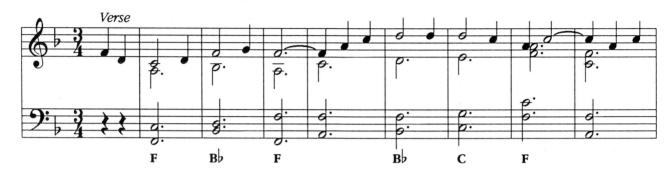

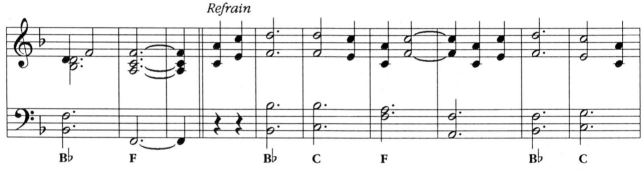

1 In a byre near Bethlehem,
   Passed by many a wand'ring stranger,
   The most precious Word of Life
   Was heard gurgling in a manger,
   For the good of us all.

   And he's here when we call him,
   Bringing health, love and laughter
   To life now and ever after,
   For the good of us all.

2 By the Galilean Lake
   Where the people flocked for teaching,
   The most precious Word of Life
   Fed their mouths as well as preaching,
   For the good of us all.

   And he's here when we call him, . . .

3 Quiet was Gethsemane,
   Camouflaging priest and soldier;
   The most precious Word of Life
   Took the world's weight on his shoulder,
   For the good of us all.

   And he's here when we call him, . . .

4 On the hill of Calvary —
  Place to end all hope of living —
  The most precious Word of Life
  Breathed his last and died, forgiving,
  For the good of us all.

  And he's here when we call him, . . .

5 In a garden, just at dawn,
  Near the grave of human violence,
  The most precious Word of Life
  Cleared his throat and ended silence,
  For the good of us all.

  And he's here when we call him, . . .

Gaelic prayers are always rich in gospel images and phrases, and this hymn from the Iona Community echoes a phrase from the great meditation opening St John's gospel: 'In the beginning was the Word, and the Word was with God, and the Word was God . . . '. The hymn tells the story of Jesus, from his birth to his death and resurrection, assuring us that the Word of Life is still here for us all.

Scottish traditional

Words and musical arrangement © 1987 Iona Community/Wild Goose Publications, Pearce Institute, Govan, Glasgow G51 3UT, Scotland (from Heaven Shall Not Wait*). Used by permission.*

44 In dulci jubilo

(F)

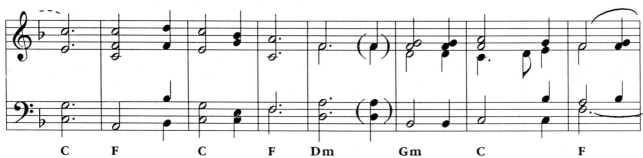
C F C F Dm Gm C F

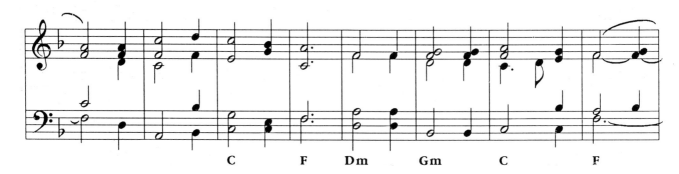
C F Dm Gm C F

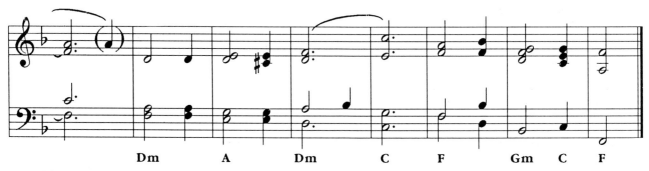
Dm A Dm C F Gm C F

1 In dulci jubilo
  Now sing we all i-o, i-o,
  He, our love, our pleasure
  Lies in praesepio,
  Like brightly gleaming treasure
  Matris in gremio:
  Alpha es et O!
  Alpha es et O!

2 O Jesu parvule,
  For you I long alway;
  Hear me in my sadness,
  O puer optime;
  With goodness and with gladness,
  O princeps gloriae,
  Trahe me post te!
  Trahe me post te!

3 O Patris caritas!
  O Nati lenitas!
  We were past reprieving
  Per nostra crimina;
  For us you are retrieving
  Coelorum gaudia,
  O that we were there!
  O that we were there!

4 Ubi sunt gaudia?
  O nowhere more than there;
  Angels there are singing
  Nova cantica,
  And there the bells are ringing
  In regis curia,
  O that we were there!
  O that we were there!

Being half in Latin and half (originally) in German, this carol is known as 'macaronic' — we suppose a mediaeval form of 'Franglais'. The original words are said to have been sung by angels to Henry Suso, the mystic, who then danced with his celestial visitors (who, incidentally, pronounced 'i-o' as 'ee-o'). This is a new translation by Geoffrey Court.

The original melody is also 14th-century. It was harmonized by Robert Lucas de Pearsall (1795–1856) and arranged here by W. J. Westbrook.

German/Latin, 14th century, tr. Geoffrey Court

45 Infant holy, infant lowly   Polish traditional melody

1. Infant holy, infant lowly,
   For his bed a cattle stall;
   Oxen lowing, little knowing
   Christ the babe is Lord of all.
   Swift are winging, angels singing,
   Nowells ringing, tidings bringing,
   Christ the babe is Lord of all,
   Christ the babe is Lord of all.

2. Flocks were sleeping, shepherds keeping
   Vigil till the morning new;
   Saw the glory, heard the story,
   Tidings of a gospel true.
   Thus rejoicing, free from sorrow,
   Praises voicing, greet the morrow,
   Christ the babe was born for you!
   Christ the babe was born for you!

This English version of a Polish carol was made in the mid-1920s by Miss Reed for Music and Youth, *and became very popular in schools.*

Little is known about the origin of the tune, although it is probably also traditional Polish.

Polish, tr. Edith M. Reed

46 *In the bleak midwinter* Cranham

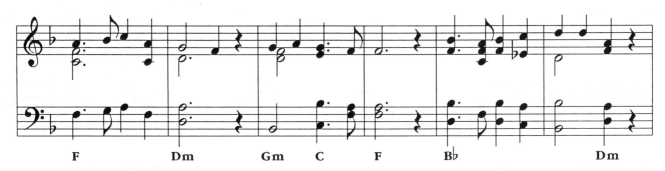
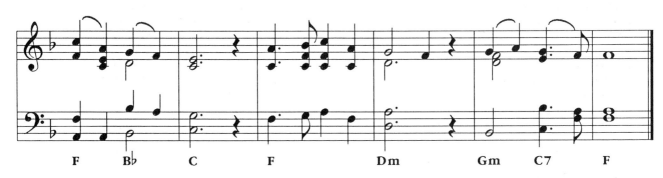

1. In the bleak midwinter
   Frosty wind made moan,
   Earth stood hard as iron,
   Water like a stone:
   Snow had fallen, snow on snow,
   Snow on snow,
   In the bleak midwinter,
   Long ago.

2. Our God, heaven cannot hold him
   Nor earth sustain;
   Heaven and earth shall flee away
   When he comes to reign:
   In the bleak midwinter
   A stable place sufficed
   The Lord God Almighty,
   Jesus Christ.

3. Enough for him, whom Cherubim
   Worship night and day,
   A breastful of milk,
   And a manger full of hay:
   Enough for him, whom angels
   Fall down before,
   The ox and ass and camel
   Which adore.

4. Angels and archangels
   May have gathered there,
   Cherubim and seraphim
   Thronged the air
   But only his mother
   In her maiden bliss
   Worshipped the Belovèd
   With a kiss.

5. What can I give him,
   Poor as I am?
   If I were a shepherd
   I would bring a lamb;
   If I were a wise man
   I would do my part;
   Yet what I can I give him:
   Give my heart.

The beautiful words are matched by Gustav Holst's simple, heart-catching tune 'Cranham'.

At first sight, the words can be difficult to fit in, especially at the beginnings of lines. It helps to notice which are the important syllables, and put those on the strong beats (in verse 2, for example, 'God', 'stable', 'Lord').

Christina Rossetti (1830–94)

47. I saw three ships come sailing in

1. I saw three ships come sailing in,
   On Christmas Day, on Christmas Day,
   I saw three ships come sailing in,
   On Christmas Day in the morning.

2. And what was in those ships all three,
   On Christmas Day, on Christmas Day,
   And what was in those ships all three,
   On Christmas Day in the morning?

3. Our Saviour Christ and his Ladie,
   On Christmas Day, on Christmas Day,
   Our Saviour Christ and his Ladie,
   On Christmas Day in the morning.

4. Pray, whither sailed those ships all three,
   On Christmas Day, on Christmas Day,
   Pray, whither sailed those ships all three,
   On Christmas Day in the morning?

5. O they sailed into Bethlehem,
   On Christmas Day, on Christmas Day,
   O they sailed into Bethlehem,
   On Christmas Day in the morning.

6. And all the bells on earth shall ring,
   On Christmas Day, on Christmas Day,
   And all the bells on earth shall ring,
   On Christmas Day in the morning.

7. And all the angels in heaven shall sing,
   On Christmas Day, on Christmas Day,
   And all the angels in heaven shall sing,
   On Christmas Day in the morning.

8. And all the souls on earth shall sing,
   On Christmas Day, on Christmas Day,
   And all the souls on earth shall sing,
   On Christmas Day in the morning.

9. Then let us all rejoice amain,
   On Christmas Day, on Christmas Day,
   Then let us all rejoice amain,
   On Christmas Day in the morning.

Another traditional folk carol that was sung all over Victorian England, sometimes in a version which begins 'As I sat on a sunny bank'. It tells a legendary story for Christmas through question and answer, and works well when the singers divide to sing alternate verses.

English traditional

48 *It came upon the midnight clear* Noël

1 It came upon the midnight clear,
   That glorious song of old,
   From angels bending near the earth
   To touch their harps of gold:
   'Peace on the earth, good-will to men,
   From heaven's all gracious King!'
   The world in solemn stillness lay
   To hear the angels sing.

2 Still through the cloven skies they come,
   With peaceful wings unfurled;
   And still their heavenly music floats
   O'er all the weary world;
   Above its sad and lowly plains
   They bend on hovering wing;
   And ever o'er its Babel sounds
   The blessèd angels sing.

3 Yet with the woes of sin and strife
   The world has suffered long;
   Beneath the angel-strain have rolled
   Two thousand years of wrong;
   And man, at war with man, hears not
   The love-song which they bring:
   O hush the noise, ye men of strife,
   And hear the angels sing!

4 For lo! the days are hastening on,
   By prophet bards foretold,
   When, with the ever-circling years,
   Comes round the age of gold;
   When peace shall over all the earth
   Its ancient splendours fling,
   And the whole world give back the song
   Which now the angels sing.

One of the few Victorian carols to emphasize the social message of Christmas: Peace on earth. It was written by an American Unitarian minister, and its powerful plea for peace came, ironically, just ten years before the American Civil War broke out.
   The tune, 'Noël', is by Arthur Sullivan (1842–1900).

Edmund Sears (1810–76)

49 *It was on a starry night (A Starry Night)*

1 It was on a starry night
  When the hills were bright,
  Earth lay sleeping, sleeping calm and still.
  Then in a cattle shed
  In a manger bed,
  A child was born King of all the world.

   And all the angels sang for him,
   The bells of heaven rang for him,
   For a child was born King of all the world.
   And all the angels sang for him,
   The bells of heaven rang for him,
   For a child was born King of all the world.

Salvation Army songster Joy Webb wrote the words and music of this carol, which is about a calm, still earth, a rejoicing heaven, shepherds who learn to believe in peace again, and a boy born to be king.

2 Soon the shepherds came that way
  Where the baby lay
  And were kneeling, kneeling by his side,
  And their hearts believed again
  For the peace of men,
  For a boy was born King of all the world.

   And all the angels sang for him, . . .

Joy Webb

Words and music © Salvationist Publishing and Supplies Ltd, London. Used by permission.

50 I warm my son upon my breast (Nkosi Jesus)

1 I warm my son upon my breast
  As Mary, Mary warmèd you,
  O, Nkosi Jesus, O, Nkosi Jesus.
  I feel his life, I feel his strength
  And his gentle quiet breathing.
  O, Nkosi Jesus, O, Nkosi Jesus.

2 I hear my people singing their song,
  Singing, singing in the wind,
  O, Nkosi Jesus, O, Nkosi Jesus.
  The sighing of the yellow grass
  Keeps him softly, sweetly dreaming.
  O, Nkosi Jesus, O, Nkosi Jesus.

3 The kaffir-boom lifts her arms above,
  Praising, praising only you,
  O, Nkosi Jesus, O, Nkosi Jesus.
  O give us your hope, O give us your strength,
  O give us, give us gentle love.
  O, Nkosi Jesus, O, Nkosi Jesus.

The story of the Nativity is seen through the eyes of an African mother. 'Nkosi' is a Zulu word for king, chief or lord. The 'kaffir-boom' is the African 'lucky-bean tree'.

This beautiful lullaby, with its exquisitely shaped melody by Edith Hugo Bosman, needs to be sung with the utmost simplicity.

Rae Tomlin

Words © Rae Tomlin. Music © Edith Hugo Bosman. Words and music used by permission of Blandford, a Cassell imprint.

51 *I wonder as I wander, out under the sky*

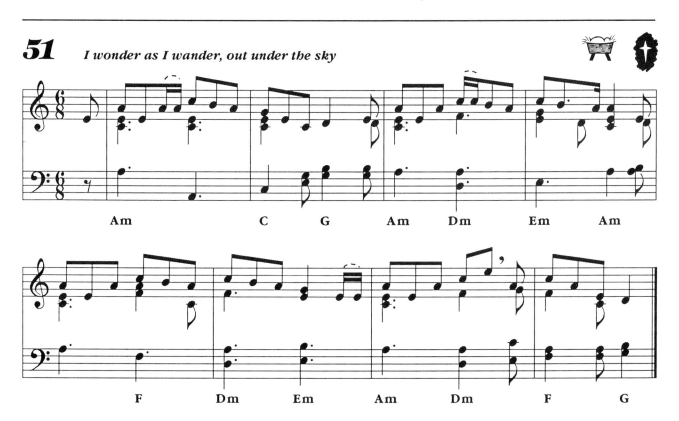

1 I wonder as I wander, out under the sky,
  How Jesus the Saviour did come for to die
  For poor or'n'ry people like you and like I . . .
  I wonder as I wander, out under the sky.

2 When Mary bore Jesus, 'twas in a cow's stall,
  With wise men and animals and shepherds and all.
  But high from the heavens a star's light did fall,
  And the promise of ages it then did recall.

3 If Jesus had wanted for any wee thing,
  A star in the sky or a bird on the wing,
  Or all of God's angels in heaven for to sing,
  He could surely have had it, 'cause he was the king.

4 I wonder as I wander, out under the sky,
  How Jesus the Saviour did come for to die
  For poor or'n'ry people like you and like I . . .
  I wonder as I wander, out under the sky.

An unusual song, written in the first person singular and often performed as a solo. The words are deliberately ungrammatical and 'rustic'; and the unresolved, unconventional tune makes a perfect match.

North Carolina traditional

52. Jesus, good above all other — Quem Pastores Laudavere

1. Jesus, good above all other,
   Gentle child of gentle mother,
   In a stable born our brother,
   Give us grace to persevere.

2. Jesus, cradled in a manger,
   For us facing every danger,
   Living as a homeless stranger,
   Make we thee our King most dear.

3. Jesus, for thy people dying,
   Risen Master, death defying,
   Lord in heaven, thy grace supplying,
   Keep us to thy presence near.

4. Jesus, who our sorrows bearest,
   All our thoughts and hopes thou sharest,
   Thou to us the truth declarest;
   Help us all thy truth to hear.

5. Lord, in all our doings guide us;
   Pride and hate shall ne'er divide us;
   We'll go on with thee beside us,
   And with joy we'll persevere!

Percy Dearmer wrote this hymn for children, to go with the 14th-century German carol tune 'Quem Pastores Laudavere', which was traditionally sung around the crib in church during the Christmas Mystery plays.

Percy Dearmer (1867–1936)

Harmonisation by Ralph Vaughan Williams (1872–1958) from the English Hymnal by permission of Oxford University Press

53. Jesus, Son of God, well-spring of forgiveness

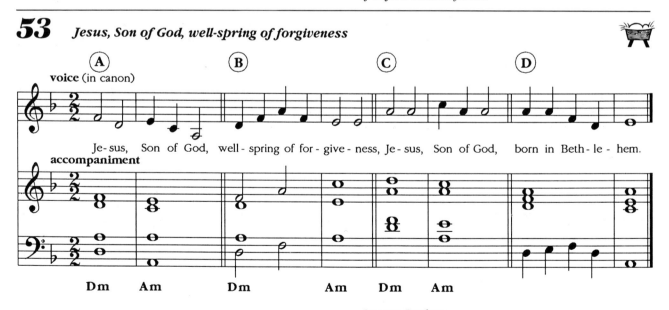

Jacques Berthier

Another four-part canon from Taizé at Christmas (see 'Gloria', no. 26).

Words and music © Ateliers et Presses de Taizé, 71250 Taizé Communauté, France. Used by permission.

54 *Jesus was born in a stable*
(Good Enough for Him)

1 Jesus was born in a stable:
　There was no room in the inn.
　He had a stall for a cradle;
　That was good enough for him.

2 Cattle asleep in the corner,
　Joseph kept watch from within.
　Can you imagine the sorrow?
　That was good enough for him.

3 No kingly robes for his vesture,
　No royal hall for this One.
　But Mary fondled her treasure,
　For he was God's dear Son.

4 Jesus was born in a stable:
　There was no room in the inn.
　He had a stall for a cradle;
　That was good enough for him.

　　And that was good enough for him.

This blues with a slow insistent rhythm is about the simple circumstances of Christ's birth.

Peter Chesters

Words and music © 1960 Joseph Weinberger Limited. Used by permission of the copyright owners.

55 Joseph, dearest Joseph mine

1 Joseph, dearest Joseph mine,
   Help me rock this child of mine;
   God will honour thee and thine
   In heav'n with him, the holy son of Mary.

   Christ was born on Christmas Day,
   On Christmas Day in Israel;
   Mary mother hears the word of Gabriel.
   Eia, Eia,
   Christ is born, the holy son of Mary.

2 Gladly will I, lady mine,
   Help to rock this child of thine;
   God's own heav'nly light shall shine
   On me and mine, from him, the son of Mary.

   Christ was born on Christmas Day, . . .

3 Peace and pardon bless us all,
   God in heaven is God in stall;
   There he lies, a babe so small,
   To ransom us, the holy son of Mary.

   Christ was born on Christmas Day, . . .

4 Thou art come to keep my heart,
   Love, th'eternal Word thou art,
   Help me now to play my part
   And welcome him, the holy son of Mary.

   Christ was born on Christmas Day, . . .

5 Sweet thou art, O Babe of Grace,
   Poor thou art, and poor thy place,
   Yet in godhead turn thy face
   To smile and save, O holy Son of Mary.

   Christ was born on Christmas Day, . . .

An imaginary conversation between Joseph and Mary. Both tune and words were written to be sung round the crib as part of a German Mystery play.

German, 15th century, tr. Elizabeth Poston

Musical arrangement by Ralph Vaughan Williams. Used by permission of Oxford University Press.

56 Joy to the world! the Lord is come — Antioch

1. Joy to the world! the Lord is come;
   Let earth receive her King;
   Let ev'ry heart prepare him room,
   And heav'n and nature sing,
   And heav'n and nature sing,
   And heav'n, and heav'n and nature sing.

2. Joy to the world! the Saviour reigns;
   Let us our songs employ;
   While fields and floods, rocks, hills and plains,
   Repeat the sounding joy,
   Repeat the sounding joy,
   Repeat, repeat the sounding joy.

3. No more let sin and sorrow grow,
   Nor thorns infest the ground;
   He comes to make his blessings flow
   Far as the curse is found,
   Far as the curse is found,
   Far as, far as the curse is found.

4. He rules the world with truth and grace,
   And makes the nations prove
   The glories of his righteousness,
   And wonders of his love,
   And wonders of his love,
   And wonders, and wonders of his love.

Isaac Watts's words and Handel's tune 'Antioch' have been enjoying a popular revival in recent years, largely through black-led churches, whose gospel choirs have made a great impact, particularly on televised gospel services, and programmes like Channel 4's People Get Ready *and BBC TV's* Rock Gospel Show.

Isaac Watts (1673–1748)

57 King Jesus hath a garden, full of divers flow'rs

1. King Jesus hath a garden, full of divers flow'rs,
   Where I go culling posies gay, all times and hours.

   There naught is heard but Paradise bird,
   Harp, dulcimer, lute, with cymbal,
   Trump and tymbal, and the tender, soothing flute;
   With cymbal, trump and tymbal,
   And the tender, soothing flute.

2. The Lily, white in blossom there, is Chastity:
   The Violet, with sweet perfume, Humility.

   There naught is heard but Paradise bird, ...

3. The bonny Damask-rose is known as Patience:
   The blithe and thrifty Marygold, Obedience.

   There naught is heard but Paradise bird, ...

4. The Crown Imperial bloometh too in yonder place,
   'Tis Charity, of stock divine, the flower of grace.

   There naught is heard but Paradise bird, ...

5. Yet, 'mid the brave, the bravest prize of all may claim
   The Star of Bethlem — Jesus — blessèd be his Name!

   There naught is heard but Paradise bird, ...

6. Ah! Jesu Lord, my heal and weal, my bliss complete,
   Make thou my heart thy garden-plot, fair, trim and neat.

   That I may hear this musick clear:
   Harp, dulcimer, lute, with cymbal,
   Trump and tymbal, and the tender, soothing flute;
   With cymbal, trump and tymbal,
   And the tender, soothing flute.

A traditional Dutch carol, harmonized by Charles Wood, naming the flowers that grow in Jesus' garden in Paradise, the spiritual virtues that are associated with them, and the musical instruments the angels are playing.

Dutch, 17th century, tr. George Ratcliffe Woodward (1848–1934)

58 *Les anges dans nos campagnes*

For the music see 'Angels, from the realms of glory', no. 5.

59 Light, scattering the darkness — Beckoning Star

1 Light, scattering the darkness,
  Shines on Christmas night;
  Wise men begin their journey,
  Following the light.

  Star, twinkling in the heavens,
  Beckon humankind:
  'Seek the Lord and you will find
  the light of the world.'

2 Light, piercing through the darkness
  Deep within us all,
  Shine clearly on our pathway;
  Guide us lest we fall.

  Star, twinkling in the heavens, . . .

3 Christ, light of every nation,
  Teach the world your ways;
  Truth, justice, love and mercy
  Make our songs of praise.

  Star, twinkling in the heavens, . . .

The light that led the wise men to Bethlehem all those years ago is still shining, and calling all of us to search for Christ today.

Patrick Appleford (b. 1925)

Words and music © Patrick Appleford 1990

60 Little donkey, little donkey

1 Little donkey, little donkey,
  On a dusty road,
  Got to keep on plodding onward
  With your precious load:

2 Been a long time, little donkey,
  Through the winter's night —
  Don't give up now, little donkey,
  Bethlehem's in sight.

    Ring out those bells tonight,
    Bethlehem, Bethlehem;
    Follow that star tonight,
    Bethlehem, Bethlehem!

3 Little donkey, little donkey,
  Had a heavy day —
  Little donkey, carry Mary
  Safely on her way.

    Little donkey, carry Mary
    Safely on her way.

Written in 1959, a song that used to make it regularly into the Top Twenty at Christmas time, particularly in the days of BBC Radio's Children's Favourites *in the 1950s and 1960s. It is printed here in G.C. Westcott's arrangement.*

Eric Boswell

Words and music © 1959 Chappell Music Ltd. Used by permission of Chappell Music Ltd and International Music Publications.

61 *Little Jesus, sweetly sleep, do not stir (Rocking)* Rocking

1 Little Jesus, sweetly sleep, do not stir;
   We will lend a coat of fur.
   We will rock you, rock you, rock you,
   We will rock you, rock you, rock you:
   See the fur to keep you warm,
   Snugly round your tiny form.

2 Mary's little baby, sleep, sweetly sleep,
   Sleep in comfort, slumber deep.
   We will rock you, rock you, rock you,
   We will rock you, rock you, rock you:
   We will serve you all we can,
   Darling, darling little man.

This traditional Czech melody, arranged here by Martin Shaw (1875–1958), is very similar to nursery rhyme tunes for 'Twinkle, twinkle, little star' and 'Baa baa black sheep', and is easily taught to very young children; but whoever sings it should do so slowly, softly and smoothly.

*Czech, tr. Percy Dearmer (1867–1936)
Musical arrangement © Martin Shaw. Used by permission of Oxford University Press.*

62 *Lo! he comes with clouds descending* Helmsley

1 Lo! he comes with clouds descending,
  Once for favoured sinners slain;
  Thousand thousand saints attending
  Swell the triumph of his train:
  Alleluya!
  Alleluya!
  Alleluya!
  God appears, on earth to reign.

2 Every eye shall now behold him
  Robed in dreadful majesty;
  Those who set at nought and sold him,
  Pierced and nailed him to the tree,
  Deeply wailing,
  Deeply wailing,
  Deeply wailing
  Shall the true Messiah see.

3 Those dear tokens of his passion
  Still his dazzling body bears,
  Cause of endless exultation
  To his ransomed worshippers:
  With what rapture,
  With what rapture,
  With what rapture
  Gaze we on those glorious scars!

4 Yea, amen! let all adore thee,
  High on thine eternal throne;
  Saviour, take the power and glory:
  Claim the kingdom for thine own:
  O come quickly!
  O come quickly!
  O come quickly!
  Alleluya! Come, Lord, come!

With his 1758 amendments, Charles Wesley toned down considerably the rather crudely passionate hymn, based on Revelation 1.7, which Cennick had written in 1750. Subsequent editors made even further revisions, but the words remain full of apocalyptic, ominous images, and have great grandeur which, combined with the tremendous tune, 'Helmsley', make this a splendid processional hymn.

J. Cennick (1718–55) and Charles Wesley (1707–88)

63 Long time ago in Bethlehem (Mary's Boy Child)

1 Long time ago in Bethlehem,
So the Holy Bible say,
Mary's boy-child, Jesus Christ,
Was born on Christmas Day.

> Hark now, hear the angels sing —
> A new king born today!
> And we may live for evermore
> Because of Christmas Day.
> Trumpets sound and angels sing —
> Listen to what they say,
> That we may live for evermore
> Because of Christmas Day.

2 While shepherds watch their flocks by night,
Them see a bright new shining star;
Them hear a choir sing —
The music seems to come from afar.

3 Now Joseph and his wife Mary
Come to Bethlehem that night;
She have no place to bear her child —
Not a single room was in sight.

> Hark now, hear the angels sing . . .

4 By and by they find a little nook
In a stable all forlorn,
And in a manger cold and dark,
Mary's little boy was born.

5 Long time ago in Bethlehem,
So the Holy Bible say,
Mary's boy-child, Jesus Christ,
Was born on Christmas Day.

> Hark now, hear the angels sing . . .

> Yes, we may live for evermore
> Because of Christmas Day.

A popular West Indian carol that has also appeared in the Top Twenty. It may need some practice, because the way the words fit the notes varies from verse to verse. One possibility would be to have the verses sung by a soloist; but in any case, this music benefits from a flexible approach to the rhythm.

The final two lines are sung to the last four-and-a-quarter bars of the refrain.

Jester Hairston

Words and music © Bourne Music Ltd. Used by permission.

---

64   *Love came down at Christmas*   Garton

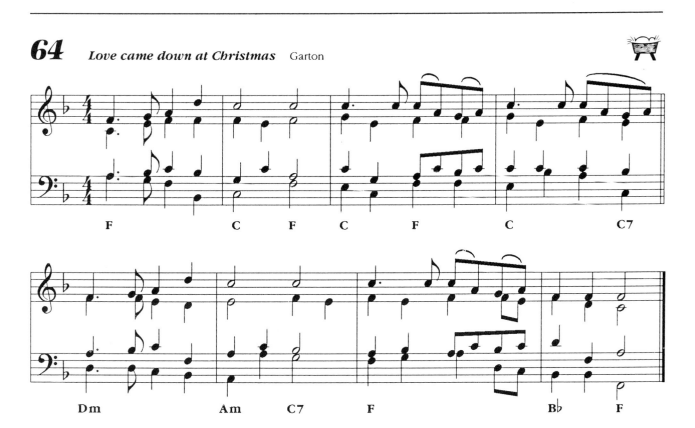

69

1 Love came down at Christmas,
   Love all lovely, love divine;
   Love was born at Christmas,
   Star and angels gave the sign.

2 Worship we the Godhead,
   Love incarnate, love divine;
   Worship we our Jesus:
   But wherewith for sacred sign?

3 Love shall be our token,
   Love be yours and love be mine;
   Love to God and neighbour,
   Love for plea and gift and sign.

Written in 1885, this is a beautiful, short hymn, best sung in unison, that says a lot in very few words.
   'Garton' is a traditional Irish air, arranged here by David Iliff.

Christina Rossetti (1830–94)

65 Lully, lulla, thou little tiny child (Coventry Carol)

Lully, lulla, thou little tiny child,
By by, lully lullay.

1 O sisters too,
   How may we do
   For to preserve this day?
   This poor youngling,
   For whom we sing,
   By by, lully lullay!

2 Herod, the king,
   In his raging,
   Chargèd he hath this day
   His men of might,
   In his own sight,
   All young children to slay.

3 That woe is me,
   Poor child for thee!
   And ever morn and may,
   For thy parting
   Neither say nor sing
   By by, lully lullay!

   Lully, lulla, thou little tiny child,
   By by, lully, lullay.

Part of the mediaeval Coventry Plays, the words and music are laden with impending doom, for all the innocent children born at this time who will be massacred by King Herod.
   The music has been arranged by Martin Shaw (1875–1958).

Pageant of the Shearmen and Tailors, Coventry, 15th century

Musical arrangement © William Elkin Music Services

66 Magnificat anima mea dominum

1 My soul proclaims the / greatness of thé Lórd
2 Because he has looked upon his / lówly hándmáid.
3 Holy / ís hís náme,
4 He has shown the / pówer of hís árm,
5 He has pulled down / prínces from théir thrónes
6 The hungry he has / filled with góod thíngs,
7 He has come to the help of / Ísrael hís sérvant,

1 And my spirit exults in / Gód my sáviour;
2 Yes, from this day forward all generations will call me blessèd, for the Almighty has done / gréat things for mé.
3 And his mercy reaches from age to age for / thóse who féar him.
4 He has routed the / próud of héart,
5 And ex- / álted the lówly.
6 The rich sent / émpty awáy.
7 Mindful of his mercy to Abraham and to his de- / scéndants for éver.

repeat Chorus except after last verse.

The Magnificat, or Song of Mary at the Visitation, is traditionally associated with our preparation for the coming of Christ. This version comes from the Taizé Community.

Jacques Berthier

© Ateliers et Presses de Taizé, 71250 Taizé Communauté, France. Used by permission.

67   *Make straight in the desert a highway for our God*   Highway

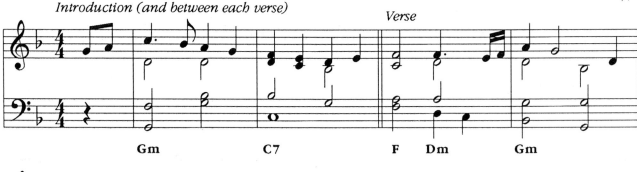

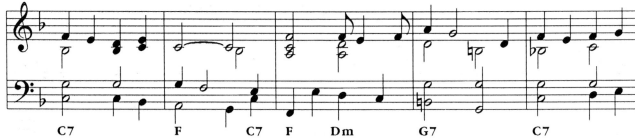

1. Make straight in the desert a highway for our God;
   John echoes Isaiah: prepare the way of the Lord.
   Look, look for his coming to set his people free;
   Christ is the Messiah whose glory all shall see.

2. Crowds flocked to the desert and found young John inspired;
   His passionate preaching made clear what God required:
   Turn, turn to the Father, and listen to his Word;
   Make straight in the desert a highway for our God.

3. Christ went to the desert and humbly was baptized.
   John witnessed the glory before his very eyes:
   Joy, joy with the Father, the Spirit and the Son,
   Signs there in the desert God's highway was begun.

4. John would not be silenced by violence or fear.
   John, murdered in prison, still speaks to those who hear:
   Learn, learn from the Baptist; hold fast to what is true;
   Make your heart a highway for God to come to you.

5. Yours, Lord, is the glory, let all your saints rejoice.
   John was the forerunner with true prophetic voice.
   Great, great is your glory, yet you come down to earth,
   Heav'n rings with the echoes of joy at Jesu's birth.

Using biblical phrases from Isaiah 40 and 61, and the story and message of John the Baptist in the gospels, Patrick Appleford's Advent hymn says: make your heart a highway for God to come to you.

Patrick Appleford (b. 1925)

Words and music © Patrick Appleford 1990

68 Make way, make way

1. Make way, make way,
   For Christ the king in splendour arrives;
   Fling wide the gates
   And welcome him into your lives.

   Make way, (make way,)
   For the King of Kings;
   Make way, (make way,)
   And let his kingdom in!

2. He comes the broken hearts to heal,
   The prisoners to free;
   The deaf shall hear, the lame shall dance,
   The blind shall see.

   Make way, (make way,) . . .

3. And those who mourn with heavy hearts,
   Who weep and sigh,
   With laughter, joy and royal crown
   He'll beautify.

   Make way, (make way,) . . .

4. We call you now to worship him
   As Lord of all,
   To have no gods before him —
   Their thrones must fall!

   Make way, (make way,) . . .

Based on Isaiah 40.3–5 and Luke 4.18–19 (see also 'Hark the glad sound!', no. 33). Graham Kendrick's lively, evangelical hymns have won renown and popularity through being broadcast regularly on television and radio.

Graham Kendrick

Words and music © Graham Kendrick/Thankyou Music. Used by permission.

69 Mary had a baby

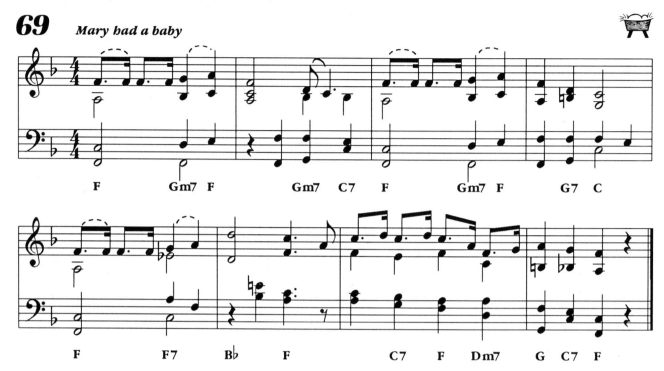

1. Mary had a baby,
    Yes, Lord.
   Mary had a baby,
    Yes, my Lord.
   Mary had a baby,
    Yes, Lord.
      The people keep a-coming
      And the train done gone.

2. What did she name him?
    Yes, Lord . . .

3. Mary named him Jesus,
    Yes, Lord . . .

4. Where was he born?
    Yes, Lord . . .

5. Born in a stable,
    Yes, Lord . . .

6. Where did Mary lay him?
    Yes, Lord . . .

7. Laid him in a manger,
    Yes, Lord . . .

A version of a traditional spiritual, and another one that children can add to, building up the Christmas story (see 'Here we go up to Bethlehem', no. 35).

The tune lends itself to accompaniment on percussion instruments.

St Helena Island spiritual

Words and music © David Iliff. Used by permission of A. & C. Black.

70 Masters in this hall

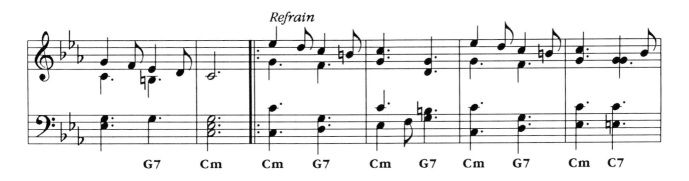
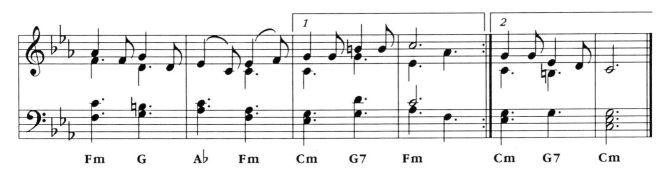

1. Masters in this hall,
   Hear ye news today
   Brought from over sea,
   And ever I you pray:

   Nowell! Nowell! Nowell!
   Nowell sing we clear!
   Holpen are all folk on earth,
   Born is God's Son so dear:
   Nowell! Nowell! Nowell!
   Nowell sing we loud!
   God today hath poor folk raised
   And cast adown the proud.

2. Going o'er the hills,
   Through the milk-white snow,
   Heard I ewès bleat
   While the wind did blow:

   Nowell! Nowell! Nowell! . . .

3. Shepherds many an one
   Sat among the sheep,
   No man spake more word
   Than they had been asleep:

   Nowell! Nowell! Nowell! . . .

4. Quoth I, 'Fellows mine,
   Why this guise sit ye?
   Making but dull cheer,
   Shepherds though ye be?

   Nowell! Nowell! Nowell! . . .

5. 'Shepherds should of right
   Leap and dance and sing,
   Thus to see ye sit,
   It is a right strange thing':

   Nowell! Nowell! Nowell! . . .

6. Quoth these fellows then,
   'To Bethlem town we go,
   To see a mighty lord
   Lie in a manger low':

   Nowell! Nowell! Nowell! . . .

7. Then to Bethlem town
   We went two and two,
   And in a sorry place
   Heard the oxen low:

   Nowell! Nowell! Nowell! . . .

8. Therein did we see
   A sweet and goodly may
   And a fair old man,
   Upon the straw she lay:

   Nowell! Nowell! Nowell! . . .

9. And a little child
   On her arm had she,
   'Wot ye who this is?'
   Said the hinds to me:

   Nowell! Nowell! Nowell! . . .

10. This is Christ the Lord,
    Masters be ye glad!
    Christmas is come in,
    And no folk should be sad:

    Nowell! Nowell! Nowell! . . .

Morris wrote these words about 1860, for an old French tune obtained at Chartres by Edmund Sedding, an architect with whom Morris was working. Sedding published the piece in his Antient Christmas Carols.

Such a long carol can be useful for a procession; the different characters can be taken by different voices or groups, with everyone joining in the chorus.

William Morris (1834–96)

71 *No crowded eastern street* Heritage

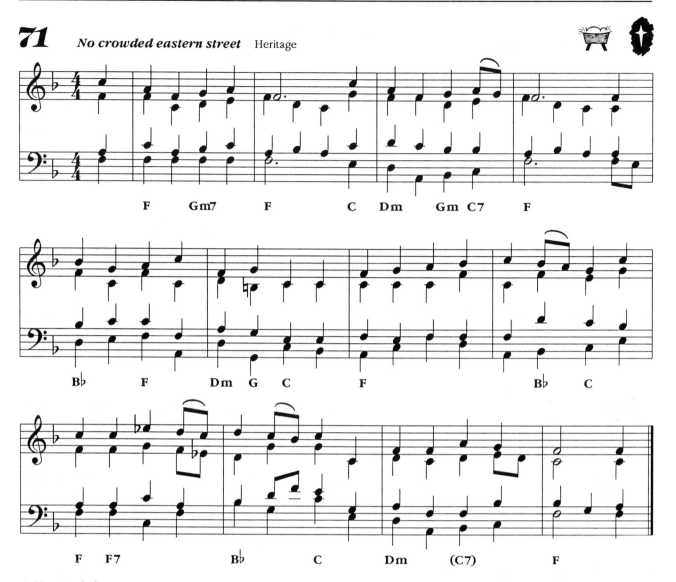

1 No crowded eastern street,
  No sound of passing feet;
  Far to the left and far to right
  The prairie snows spread fair and white;
  Yet still to us is born tonight
  The child, the King of Glory.

2 No rock-hewn place of peace
  Shared with the gentle beasts,
  But sturdy farmhouse, stout and warm,
  With stable, shed and great red barn;
  And still to us is born tonight
  The child, the King of Glory.

3 No blaze of heavenly fire,
  No bright celestial choir:
  Only the starlight as of old,
  Crossed by the planes' flash, red and gold;
  Yet still to us is born tonight
  The child, the King of Glory.

4 No kings with gold and grain,
  No stately camel train;
  Yet in his presence all may stand
  With loving heart and willing hand;
  For still to us is born tonight
  The child, the King of Glory.

A Canadian carol, simple and effective, which places the Christmas story firmly in the 20th century.
  'Heritage' is by Robert J. B. Fleming (b. 1921).

Frieda Major (b. 1891)

72. Now the holly bears a berry as white as the milk (Sans Day Carol)

1. Now the holly bears a berry as white as the milk,
   And Mary bore Jesus, who was wrapped up in silk:

   And Mary bore Jesus Christ
   Our Saviour for to be,
   And the first tree in the greenwood,
   It was the holly, holly! holly!
   And the first tree in the greenwood,
   It was the holly.

2. Now the holly bears a berry as green as the grass,
   And Mary bore Jesus, who died on the cross:

   And Mary bore Jesus Christ . . .

3. Now the holly bears a berry as black as the coal,
   And Mary bore Jesus, who died for us all:

   And Mary bore Jesus Christ . . .

4. Now the holly bears a berry, as blood is it red,
   Then trust we our Saviour, who rose from the dead:

   And Mary bore Jesus Christ . . .

Called the Sans Day Carol after the place where it was found, St Day, in Cornwall, named after a Breton saint whose cult had spread there. The Cornish words and tune were known at St Day for years before they were discovered, collected, translated and published.

Cornish traditional, collated Percy Dearmer (1867–1936)

73 O come, all ye faithful — Adeste Fideles

1. O come, all ye faithful,
   Joyful and triumphant,
   O come ye, O come ye to Bethlehem;
   Come and behold him
   Born the King of Angels:

   O come, let us adore him,
   O come, let us adore him,
   O come, let us adore him, Christ the Lord!

2. God of God,
   Light of Light,
   Lo! he abhors not the Virgin's womb;
   Very God,
   Begotten, not created:

   O come, let us adore him, . . .

3. See how the shepherds,
   Summoned to his cradle,
   Leaving their flocks, draw nigh with lowly fear;
   We too will thither
   Bend our joyful footsteps:

   O come, let us adore him, . . .

4. Lo! star-led chieftains,
   Magi, Christ adoring,
   Offer him incense, gold, and myrrh;
   We to the Christ Child
   Bring our heart's oblations:

   O come, let us adore him, . . .

5 Child, for us sinners
  Poor and in the manger,
  Fain we embrace thee, with awe and love;
  Who would not love thee,
  Loving us so dearly?

   O come, let us adore him, . . .

6 Sing, choirs of angels,
  Sing in exultation,
  Sing, all ye citizens of heaven above;
  Glory to God
  In the Highest:

   O come, let us adore him, . . .

7 Yea, Lord, we greet thee,
  Born this happy morning,
  Jesu, to thee be glory given;
  Word of the Father,
  Now in flesh appearing:

   O come, let us adore him, . . .

Neither the irregular metre of the lines nor the lack of rhyme has prevented this carol from becoming one of the most popular of all, especially with its affirmative final verse, traditionally only sung on Christmas day itself (though on another day, it is always possible to sing 'Born that *happy morning').*

'Adeste Fideles' is by an unknown composer, but very possibly it was also by John Wade, who wrote the original Latin words.

John Francis Wade (1711–86), tr. Frederick Oakley (1802–80) and others

74 O come, O come, Emmanuel   Veni Immanuel

1 O come, O come, Emmanuel,
   And ransom captive Israel,
   That mourns in lonely exile here,
   Until the Son of God appear.

   Rejoice! Rejoice! Emmanuel
   Shall come to thee, O Israel.

2 O come, thou Rod of Jesse, free
   Thine own from Satan's tyranny;
   From depths of hell thy people save,
   And give them victory o'er the grave.

   Rejoice! Rejoice! Emmanuel . . .

3 O come, thou Dayspring, come and cheer
   Our spirits by thine advent here;
   Disperse the gloomy clouds of night,
   And death's dark shadows put to flight.

   Rejoice! Rejoice! Emmanuel . . .

4 O come, thou Key of David, come,
   And open wide our heavenly home;
   Make safe the way that leads on high,
   And close the path to misery.

   Rejoice! Rejoice! Emmanuel . . .

5 O come, O come, thou Lord of Might,
   Who to thy tribes, on Sinai's height,
   In ancient times didst give the law
   In cloud and majesty and awe.

   Rejoice! Rejoice! Emmanuel . . .

Words based on the ancient Advent antiphons of the mediaeval Church, with each verse addressing Christ by a different Old Testament title.
   'Veni Immanuel', arranged here by Noël Tredinnick, strongly suggests plainsong, and is more effective sung lightly, following the natural rhythm of the spoken word, rather than in stiff regular measures.

Latin, c. 13th century, tr. John Mason Neale (1818–66)

Musical arrangement © Noel Tredinnick/Jubilate Hymns. Used by permission.

75 *Of the Father's heart begotten* Divinum Mysterium

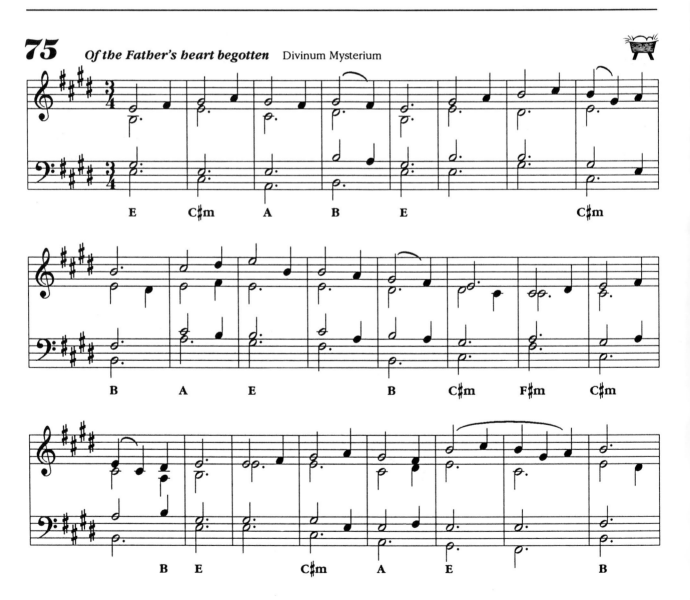

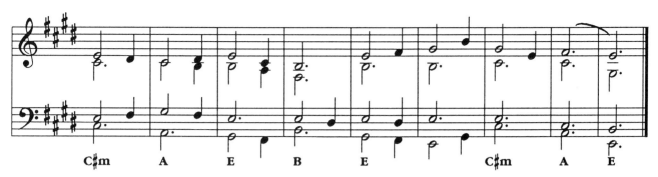

1. Of the Father's heart begotten,
   Ere the world from chaos rose,
   He is Alpha: from that fountain
   All that is and hath been flows;
   He is Omega, of all things
   Yet to come the mystic close,
   Evermore and evermore.

2. By his word was all created;
   He commanded and 'twas done;
   Earth and sky and boundless ocean,
   Universe of three in one,
   All that sees the moon's soft radiance,
   All that breathes beneath the sun,
   Evermore and evermore.

3. He assumed this mortal body,
   Frail and feeble, doomed to die,
   That the race from dust created
   Might not perish utterly,
   Which the dreadful law had sentenced
   In the depths of hell to lie,
   Evermore and evermore.

4. This is he, whom seer and sibyl
   Sang in ages long gone by;
   This is he of old revealèd
   In the page of prophecy;
   Lo! he comes, the promised saviour;
   Let the world his praises cry!
   Evermore and evermore.

5. Let the storm and summer sunshine,
   Gliding stream and sounding shore,
   Sea and forest, frost and zephyr,
   Day and night their Lord adore;
   Let creation join to laud thee
   Through the ages evermore,
   Evermore and evermore.

6. Sing, ye heights of heaven, his praises;
   Angels and archangels, sing!
   Wheresoe'er ye be, ye faithful,
   Let your joyous anthems ring,
   Every tongue his name confessing,
   Countless voices answering,
   Evermore and evermore . . .

The oldest of all Christmas hymns, often used as a processional. It is not just about Christ's Incarnation, but is a triumphant assertion of his glory and oneness with God, and all creation is invited to join in praise.

'Divinum Mysterium' is a mediaeval melody found in Piae Cantiones *(1582). It is best sung in unison, and moderately fast.*

Prudentius (348–413), tr. R. F. Davis (1866–1937)

Musical arrangement © David Iliff/Jubilate Hymns. Used by permission.

76 *O leave your sheep* Angevin

1 O leave your sheep,
   Where ewes with lambs are feeding;
   You shepherds, hear
   Our message of good cheer.
   No longer weep;
   The angel tidings heeding,
   To Bethlem haste away.
   Our Lord, (our Lord,)
   Our Lord, (our Lord,)
   Our Lord is born this happy day.
   Our Lord, (our Lord,)
   Our Lord, (our Lord,)
   Our Lord is born this happy day.

2 For love lies there
   Within a lowly manger —
   The infant poor
   Whom angel hosts adore!
   Such perfect care
   Has saved us all from danger
   And brought us to the fold.
   Now see, (now see,)
   Now see, (now see,)
   God's faithful love revealed of old.
   Now see, (now see,)
   Now see, (now see,)
   God's faithful love revealed of old.

3 You wise men three,
 Arrayed in royal splendour,
 True homage pay:
 Your king is born today!
 The star you see
 Its radiance must surrender
 Before our sun most bright.
 Your gifts, (your gifts,)
 Your gifts, (your gifts,)
 Your gifts are precious in his sight.
 Your gifts, (your gifts,)
 Your gifts, (your gifts,)
 Your gifts are precious in his sight.

4 O Spirit blessed,
 The source of life eternal,
 Our souls inspire
 With your celestial fire!
 We make our guest
 The Christ, the Lord supernal,
 And sing the peace on earth
 God gives, (God gives,)
 God gives, (God gives,)
 God gives us by this holy birth.
 God gives, (God gives,)
 God gives, (God gives,)
 God gives us by this holy birth.

An English version of the traditional French carol 'Quittez, pasteurs'. In the last six lines of each verse, the words in brackets may be sung by a second part.

'Angevin' first appeared in print in the 19th century. It needs to be sung smoothly, with the long notes given their full value, but to keep moving.

John Rutter, from the French

77 *O little one sweet, O little one mild* Jesulein Süss

1 O little one sweet, O little one mild
  Your father's purpose you have fulfilled;
  That we might understand his care
  Our fragile human life you share,
  O little one sweet, O little one mild.

2 O little one sweet, O little one mild
  With joy you have the whole world filled;
  You came to us from heaven's domain,
  To bring us comfort in our pain,
  O little one sweet, O little one mild.

3 O little one sweet, O little one mild,
  In you love's beauties are distilled;
  Then light in us your love's bright flame
  That we may give you back the same,
  O little one sweet, O little one mild.

A German carol which first appeared in 1650; a hymn of praise and prayer to the baby in the manger. Here it is in a new translation.

Harmonized as a chorale by Johann Sebastian Bach, it should be sung slowly and gently.

Samuel Scheidt (1587–1654), tr. Patrick Appleford

78 O little town of Bethlehem Forest Green (The Ploughboy's Dream)

1. O little town of Bethlehem,
   How still we see thee lie!
   Above thy deep and dreamless sleep
   The silent stars go by.
   Yet in thy dark streets shineth
   The everlasting light;
   The hopes and fears of all the years
   Are met in thee to-night.

2. O morning stars, together
   Proclaim the holy birth,
   And praises sing to God the King,
   And peace to all on earth;
   For Christ is born of Mary;
   And, gathered all above,
   While mortals sleep, the angels keep
   Their watch of wondering love.

3. How silently, how silently,
   The wondrous gift is given!
   So God imparts to human hearts
   The blessings of his heaven.
   No ear may hear his coming;
   But in this world of sin,
   Where meek souls will receive him, still
   The dear Christ enters in.

4. Where children pure and happy
   Pray to the blessèd Child,
   Where misery cries out to thee,
   Son of the mother mild;
   Where charity stands watching
   And faith holds wide the door,
   The dark night wakes, the glory breaks,
   And Christmas comes once more.

5. O holy child of Bethlehem,
   Descend to us, we pray;
   Cast out our sin, and enter in,
   Be born in us today.
   We hear the Christmas angels
   The great glad tidings tell:
   O come to us, abide with us,
   Our Lord Emmanuel.

Phillips Brooks, a great American preacher, wrote this carol for his Sunday School children. The words stir up, even in the most cynical of us, deep feelings of hope that the Christmas story should be true.

'Forest Green' is the name given by Ralph Vaughan Williams to the traditional English tune 'The Ploughboy's Dream', which matches the words perfectly. In each verse, the first note of the penultimate line is longer than many people think!

Phillips Brooks (1835–93)

Musical arrangement by Ralph Vaughan Williams. Used by permission of Oxford University Press.

79 — O Mary most holy (Lourdes Hymn)
Lourdes (Massabielle)

1. O Mary most holy, you brought forth God's Son;
   Your joy is the joy of all ages to come.

   Ave, ave, ave Maria,
   Ave, ave, ave Maria.

2. To you, by an angel, the Father made known
   The grace of his Spirit, the gift of his Son.

   Ave, ave, ave Maria, . . .

3. Your child is the Saviour, all hope lies in him:
   He gives us new life and redeems us from sin.

   Ave, ave, ave Maria, . . .

4. In glory for ever now close to your Son,
   All ages will praise you for all God has done.

   Ave, ave, ave Maria, . . .

A Nativity hymn from Lourdes, France. Pilgrims in their thousands visit the grotto where, in 1858, Bernadette Soubirous had visions of the Blessed Virgin Mary, and a spring of healing water appeared. Sung in procession by children dressed in white, the hymn is also associated with first communions.

The tune is a traditional French melody, heard on carillons everywhere around Lourdes.

The Venerable Bede, tr. and paraphrased

80. Once in royal David's city — Irby

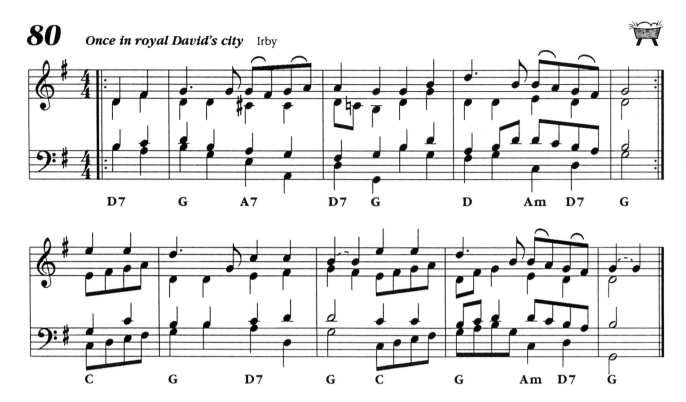

1. Once in royal David's city
   Stood a lowly cattle shed,
   Where a mother laid her baby
   In a manger for his bed:
   Mary was that mother mild,
   Jesus Christ her little child.

2. He came down to earth from heaven
   Who is God and Lord of all,
   And his shelter was a stable,
   And his cradle was a stall:
   With the poor and mean and lowly,
   Lived on earth our Saviour holy.

3. And through all his wondrous childhood
   Day by day like us he grew;
   He was little, weak and helpless,
   Tears and smiles like us he knew:
   And he feeleth for our sadness,
   And he shareth in our gladness.

4. And our eyes at last shall see him
   Through his own redeeming love,
   For that child so dear and gentle
   Is our Lord in heaven above:
   And he leads his children on
   To the place where he is gone.

5. Not in that poor lowly stable,
   With the oxen standing by,
   We shall see him: but in heaven,
   Set at God's right hand on high,
   Where like stars his children crowned,
   All in white shall wait around.

Not written by Mrs Alexander as a Christmas carol, but to illustrate part of the Apostles' Creed in her Hymns for Little Children *(1848). A skilful mingling of Bible story and Christian theology, it has become a traditional part of Christmas, partly through being chosen by Eric Milner-White to begin his especially devised Festival of Nine Lessons and Carols from King's College. This gift to the townspeople of Cambridge is now a gift to a far wider audience, broadcast live on BBC Radio every Christmas for over fifty years.*

The tune 'Irby', by H. G. Gauntlett, has been harmonized by A. H. Mann (1850–1929).

C. F. Alexander (1818–95)

81. On Christmas night, all Christians sing (Sussex Carol)

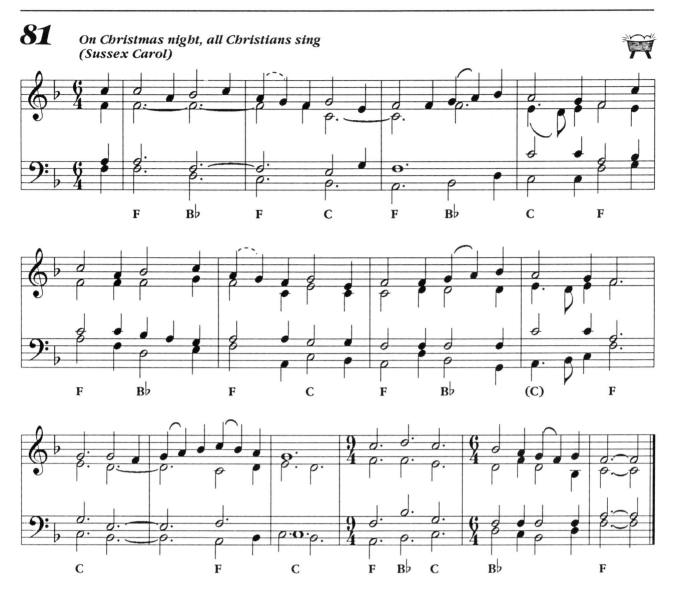

1. On Christmas night, all Christians sing
   To hear the news the angels bring:
   On Christmas night, all Christians sing
   To hear the news the angels bring:
   News of great joy, news of great mirth,
   News of our merciful King's birth.

2. Then why should we on earth be so sad,
   Since our Redeemer made us glad?
   Then why should we on earth be so sad,
   Since our Redeemer made us glad?
   When from our sin he set us free,
   All for to gain our liberty.

3. When sin departs before his grace,
   Then life and health come in its place;
   When sin departs before his grace
   Then life and health come in its place;
   Angels and we with joy may sing,
   All for to see the new-born King.

4. All out of darkness we have light,
   Which made the angels sing this night;
   All out of darkness we have light,
   Which made the angels sing this night;
   'Glory to God and peace to men,
   Now and for evermore. Amen.'

A folk carol, collected by Vaughan Williams at Monks Gate in Sussex, whose direct simplicity emphasizes the happiness we should all feel at the birth of the bringer of mercy and redemption.

Sussex traditional, collected by Ralph Vaughan Williams (1872–1958)

82 On Jordan's bank the Baptist's cry — Winchester New

1. On Jordan's bank the Baptist's cry
   Announces that the Lord is nigh;
   Come then and hearken, for he brings
   Glad tidings from the King of Kings.

2. Then cleansed be every Christian breast,
   And furnished for so great a guest!
   Yea, let us each our hearts prepare
   For Christ to come and enter there.

3. For thou art our salvation, Lord,
   Our refuge and our great reward;
   Without thy grace our souls must fade,
   And wither like a flower decayed.

4. To heal the sick stretch out thine hand,
   And bid the fallen sinner stand;
   Shine forth, and let thy light restore
   Earth's own true loveliness once more.

5. All praise, eternal Son, to thee
   Whose advent sets thy people free,
   Whom, with the Father, we adore,
   And Spirit blest, for evermore.

Written in Latin for Charles Coffin's Paris Breviary, *this hymn takes John the Baptist's call to the people of Israel to repent and prepare for Christ's coming, and addresses it to us, as we prepare for Christmas.*

'Winchester New' is adapted from a chorale in the Musikalisches Handbuch *(Hamburg 1690).*

Charles Coffin (1676–1749), tr. John Chandler (1806–76)

83 O Tannenbaum! O Tannenbaum!

1. O Tannenbaum! O Tannenbaum!
   Wie grün sind deine Blätter!
   O Tannenbaum! O Tannenbaum!
   Wie grün sind deine Blätter!
   Du grünst nicht nur zur Sommerzeit:
   Nein, auch im Winter, wenn es schneit.
   O Tannenbaum! O Tannenbaum!
   Wie grün sind deine Blätter.

2. O Tannenbaum! O Tannenbaum!
   Du kannst mir sehr gefallen!
   O Tannenbaum! O Tannenbaum!
   Du kannst mir sehr gefallen!
   Wie oft hat nicht zur Weihnachtszeit
   Ein Baum von dir mich hoch erfreit:
   O Tannenbaum! O Tannenbaum!
   Du kannst mir sehr gefallen!

3. O Tannenbaum! O Tannenbaum!
   Dein Kleid will mich was lehren!
   O Tannenbaum! O Tannenbaum!
   Dein Kleid will mich was lehren!
   Die Hoffnung und Beständigkeit
   Gibt Trost und Kraft zu jeder Zeit.
   O Tannenbaum! O Tannenbaum!
   Dein Kleid will mich was lehren!

For anyone with German roots, Christmas is not Christmas without this carol, which first appeared in the 19th century.

The tune has become associated with the words of 'The Red Flag' but it is with this traditional German carol that it originally belongs.

German traditional

84 *O worship the Lord in the beauty of holiness!* Was Lebet

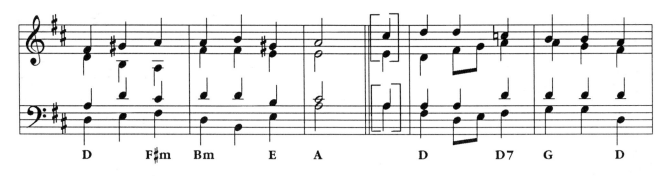
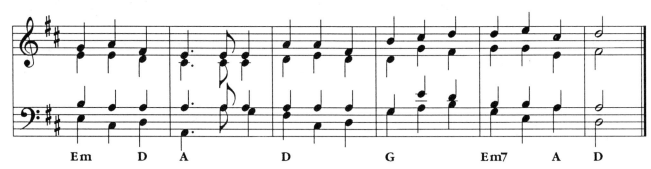

1 O worship the Lord in the beauty of holiness!
  Bow down before him, his glory proclaim;
  With gold of obedience, and incense of lowliness,
  Kneel and adore him, the Lord is his name!

2 Low at his feet lay thy burden of carefulness,
  High on his heart he will bear it for thee,
  Comfort thy sorrows, and answer thy prayerfulness,
  Guiding thy steps as may best for thee be.

3 Fear not to enter his courts in the slenderness
  Of the poor wealth thou wouldst reckon as thine:
  Truth in its beauty, and love in its tenderness,
  These are the offerings to lay on his shrine.

4 These, though we bring them in trembling and fearfulness,
  He will accept for the name that is dear;
  Mornings of joy give for evenings of tearfulness,
  Trust for our trembling and hope for our fear.

5 O worship the Lord in the beauty of holiness!
  Bow down before him, his glory proclaim;
  With gold of obedience, and incense of lowliness,
  Kneel and adore him, the Lord is his name.

Many of the poetic allusions are biblical (see Psalm 96.9; Philippians 4.6 and Psalm 30.5). The gifts are given a different interpretation from that of the early Church (see no. 11, 'Bethlehem, of noble cities'), but like Heber's, in 'Brightest and best of the sons of the morning' (no. 12), Monsell's purpose is to teach us to worship God in the right way.

'Was Lebet' is an 18th-century chorale.

J. S. B. Monsell (1811–75)

85 Past three a clock — London Waits

Past three a clock,
And a cold frosty morning:
Past three a clock;
Good morrow, masters all!

1 Born is a baby,
Gentle as may be,
Son of th'eternal
Father supernal.

Past three a clock, . . .

2 Seraph quire singeth,
Angel bell ringeth:
Hark how they rime it,
Time it, and chime it.

Past three a clock, . . .

3 Mid earth rejoices
Hearing such voices
Ne'ertofore so well
Carolling Nowell.

Past three a clock, . . .

4 Hinds o'er the pearly
Dewy lawn early
Seek the high stranger
Laid in the manger.

Past three a clock, . . .

5 Cheese from the dairy
Bring they for Mary,
And, not for money,
Butter and honey.

Past three a clock, . . .

6 Light out of star-land
Leadeth from far land
Princes, to meet him,
Worship and greet him.

Past three a clock, . . .

7 Myrrh from full coffer,
Incense they offer:
Nor is the golden
Nugget withholden.

Past three a clock, . . .

8 Thus they: I pray you,
Up, sirs, nor stay you
Till ye confess him
Likewise, and bless him.

Past three a clock, . . .

Deep mystery and familiar, homely things are described side by side in this quaint Victorian restoration of a more ancient carol.

The tune is the traditional English carol melody 'London Waits'.

George Ratcliffe Woodward (1848–1934)
(refrain traditional)

86. People, look East. The time is near
Besançon Carol

1. People, look East. The time is near
   Of the crowning of the year.
   Make your house fair as you are able,
   Trim the hearth, and set the table.
   People, look East, and sing today:
   Love the Guest is on the way.

2. Furrows, be glad. Though earth is bare,
   One more seed is planted there:
   Give up your strength the seed to nourish,
   That in course the flower may flourish.
   People, look East, and sing today:
   Love the Rose is on the way.

3. Birds, though ye long have ceased to build,
   Guard the nest that must be filled.
   Even the hour when wings are frozen
   He for fledging-time has chosen.
   People, look East, and sing today:
   Love the Bird is on the way.

4. Stars, keep the watch. When night is dim
   One more light the bowl shall brim,
   Shining beyond the frosty weather,
   Bright as sun and moon together.
   People, look East, and sing today:
   Love the Star is on the way.

5. Angels, announce to man and beast
   Him who cometh from the East.
   Set every peak and valley humming
   With the word, the Lord is coming.
   People, look East, and sing today:
   Love the Lord is on the way.

The poet Eleanor Farjeon rewrote and improved on an earlier version of the old Besançon carol 'Chantons, bargies, Noué, Noué' which began:
   'Shepherds, shake off your drowsy sleep,
   Rise, and leave your silly sheep!'

Eleanor Farjeon (1881–1965)

Words © Oxford University Press. Used by permission.

87. Rejoice and be merry in songs and in mirth
(Gallery Carol)

1. Rejoice and be merry in songs and in mirth,
   O praise our Redeemer, all mortals on earth:
   For this is the birthday of Jesus our King,
   Who brought us salvation — his praises we'll sing!

2. A heavenly vision appeared in the sky,
   Vast numbers of angels the shepherds did spy,
   Proclaiming the birthday of Jesus our King,
   Who brought us salvation — his praises we'll sing!

3. Likewise a bright star in the sky did appear,
   Which led the Wise Men from the East to draw near;
   They found the Messiah, sweet Jesus our King,
   Who brought us salvation — his praises we'll sing!

4. And when they were come, they their treasures unfold,
   And unto him offered myrrh, incense, and gold.
   So blessèd for ever be Jesus our King,
   Who brought us salvation — his praises we'll sing!

The words and tune were found in an old handwritten church gallery-book in Dorset by the Rev. L. J. T. Darwall. Much of the west gallery music disappeared when, during the 19th century, organs replaced gallery bands (about which Thomas Hardy wrote, nostalgically, in Under the Greenwood Tree*).*

Old church gallery-book

88. See amid the winter's snow — Humility

1. See amid the winter's snow,
   Born for us on earth below;
   See the tender Lamb appears,
   Promised from eternal years:

   Hail, thou ever-blessèd morn;
   Hail, redemption's happy dawn;
   Sing through all Jerusalem,
   Christ is born in Bethlehem.

2. Lo, within a manger lies
   He who built the starry skies;
   He who, throned in height sublime,
   Sits amid the cherubim:

   Hail, thou ever-blessèd morn; . .

3. Say, ye holy shepherds, say
   What your joyful news to-day;
   Wherefore have ye left your sheep
   On the lonely mountain steep?

   Hail, thou ever-blessèd morn; . . .

4. 'As we watched at dead of night,
   Lo, we saw a wondrous light;
   Angels singing "Peace on earth"
   Told us of the Saviour's birth':

   Hail, thou ever-blessèd morn; . . .

5. Sacred infant, all divine,
   What a tender love was thine,
   Thus to come from highest bliss
   Down to such a world as this:

   Hail, thou ever-blessèd morn; . . .

6. Teach, O teach us, holy child,
   By thy face so meek and mild,
   Teach us to resemble thee,
   In thy sweet humility:

   Hail, thou ever-blessèd morn; . . .

The first two verses are an expression of wonder at the way God's eternal promises are kept by a humble baby in a manger. The next two are a conversation with the rejoicing shepherds, and the last two address the holy child and ask him to teach us to be like him.
  'Humility', by John Goss (1800–80), appeared with these words in 1871.

Edward Caswall (1814–78)

89 See him lying on a bed of straw (Calypso Carol)

1. See him lying on a bed of straw:
   A draughty stable with an open door,
   Mary cradling the babe she bore —
   The Prince of Glory is his name:

   O now carry me to Bethlehem
   To see the Lord of love again:
   Just as poor as was the stable then,
   The Prince of Glory when he came.

2. Star of silver, sweep across the skies,
   Show where Jesus in the manger lies.
   Shepherds, swiftly from your stupor rise
   To see the Saviour of the world:

   O now carry me to Bethlehem . . .

3. Angels, sing again the song you sang,
   Sing the glory of God's gracious plan;
   Sing that Bethl'em's little baby can
   Be the saviour of us all:

   O now carry me to Bethlehem . . .

4 Mine are riches, from your poverty,
 From your innocence, eternity;
 Mine forgiveness by your death for me,
 Child of sorrow for my joy:

  O now carry me to Bethlehem . . .

Michael A. Perry

Words and music © 1969 Michael Perry/Jubilate Hymns.
Used by permission.

90   *Shepherds in the field abiding*

For the music see 'Angels, from the realms of glory', no. 5.

91   *Silent night, holy night!*   Stille Nacht

1 Silent night, holy night!
 All is calm, all is bright
 Round yon virgin mother and child.
 Holy infant so tender and mild,
 Sleep in heavenly peace,
 Sleep in heavenly peace.

2 Silent night, holy night!
 Shepherds quake at the sight:
 Glories stream from heaven afar,
 Heavenly hosts sing: Alleluia,
 Christ the Saviour is born!
 Christ the Saviour is born!

3 Silent night, holy night!
 Son of God, love's pure light,
 Radiance beams from thy holy face
 With the dawn of redeeming grace,
 Jesus, Lord, at thy birth,
 Jesus, Lord, at thy birth.

Franz Gruber composed this haunting tune for the newly written German words (no. 94) on Christmas Eve in 1818; when it was sung that same night, it was accompanied only by a guitar, because by a piece of poetic synchronization, the organ had broken down, making the night silent indeed.

Joseph Mohr, (1792-1884), tr. Anon.

Musical arrangement © W. L. Reed. Used by permission of Blandford, a Cassell imprint.

For a translation of the three additional verses discovered in 1997, see page 128.

94 — Stille Nacht, heilige Nacht!

1 Stille Nacht, heilige Nacht!
Alles schläft, einsam wacht
Nur das traute, hochheilige Paar.
Holder Knabe im lockigen Haar,
Schlaf' in himmlischer Ruh,
Schlaf' in himmlischer Ruh!

2 Stille Nacht, heilige Nacht!
Hirten erst kundgemacht,
Durch der Engel Halleluja
Tönt es laut von fern und nah:
Christ, der Retter, ist da,
Christ, der Retter, ist da!

3 Stille Nacht, heilige Nacht!
Gottes Sohn, O wie lacht
Lieb' aus deinem göttlichen Mund,
Da uns schlägt die rettende Stund,
Christ, in deiner Geburt,
Christ, in deiner Geburt!

The original German version of no. 91.

Joseph Mohr (1792–1884)

92 — Sing lullaby! (The Infant King)

1 Sing lullaby!
  Lullaby baby, now reclining,
  Sing lullaby!
  Hush, do not wake the Infant King.
  Angels are watching, stars are shining
  Over the place where he is lying:
  Sing lullaby!

2 Sing lullaby!
  Lullaby baby, now a-sleeping,
  Sing lullaby!
  Hush, do not wake the Infant King.
  Soon will come sorrow with the morning,
  Soon will come bitter grief and weeping:
  Sing lullaby!

3 Sing lullaby!
  Lullaby baby, now a-dozing,
  Sing lullaby!
  Hush, do not wake the Infant King.
  Soon comes the cross, the nails, the piercing,
  Then in the grave at last reposing:
  Sing lullaby!

4 Sing lullaby!
  Lullaby! is the babe a-waking?
  Sing lullaby!
  Hush, do not stir the Infant King.
  Dreaming of Easter, gladsome morning,
  Conquering death, its bondage breaking:
  Sing lullaby!

Sabine Baring-Gould wrote most of his best-known hymns for children, like 'Onward Christian soldiers', at Horbury Bridge, where he was curate. This lullaby contrasts the sweetly sleeping baby with the sorrow and bitterness that lie ahead of him, but ends rejoicing that on Easter morning he will conquer death.
The tune is a Basque noël.

Sabine Baring-Gould (1834–1924)

93 *Sing this night, for a boy is born in Bethlehem (Star Carol)*

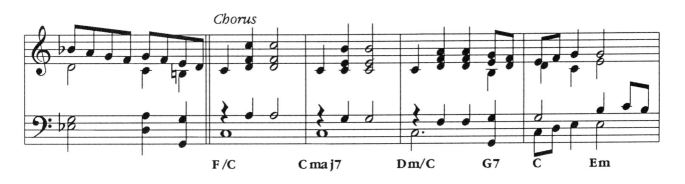

1 Sing this night, for a boy is born in Bethlehem,
  Christ our Lord in a lowly manger lies;
  Bring your gifts, come and worship at his cradle,
  Hurry to Bethlehem and see the son of Mary!

  See his star shining bright
  In the sky this Christmas night!
  Follow me joyfully;
  Hurry to Bethlehem and see the son of Mary!

2 Angels bright, come from heaven's highest glory,
  Bear the news with its message of good cheer:
  'Sing, rejoice, for a King is come to save us,
  Hurry to Bethlehem and see the son of Mary!'

  See his star shining bright . . .

3 See, he lies in his mother's tender keeping;
  Jesus Christ in her loving arms asleep.
  Shepherds poor, come to worship and adore him,
  Offer their humble gifts before the son of Mary.

  See his star shining bright . . .

4 Let us all pay our homage at the manger,
  Sing his praise on this joyful Christmas night;
  Christ is come, bringing promise of salvation;
  Hurry to Bethlehem and see the son of Mary!

  See his star shining bright . . .

Although, like 'Deep peace of the running wave to you' (no. 21), this would normally be too difficult for an untrained congregation or group of carol singers to tackle, John Rutter has made a simplified arrangement for this book.

This is one of several works which have broken through from the exclusive world of four-part choirs to that of congregational hymn-singing through popular broadcasting.

John Rutter

Words and music © John Rutter. Used by permission of Oxford University Press.

---

94 *Stille Nacht, heilige Nacht!*

For the music see 'Silent Night', no. 91.

95. Tell out, my soul, the greatness of the Lord — Woodlands

1. Tell out, my soul, the greatness of the Lord:
   Unnumbered blessings, give my spirit voice;
   Tender to me the promise of his word;
   In God my Saviour shall my heart rejoice.

2. Tell out, my soul, the greatness of his name:
   Make known his might, the deeds his arm has done;
   His mercy sure, from age to age the same;
   His holy name, the Lord, the Mighty One.

3. Tell out, my soul, the greatness of his might:
   Powers and dominions lay their glory by;
   Proud hearts and stubborn wills are put to flight,
   The hungry fed, the humble lifted high.

4. Tell out, my soul, the glories of his word:
   Firm is his promise, and his mercy sure.
   Tell out, my soul, the greatness of the Lord
   To children's children and for evermore.

A paraphrase of the New English Bible version of the Magnificat in St Luke's gospel, this hymn has won wide acceptance, and has a good tune, 'Woodlands', written in 1919 by Walter Greatorex (1877–1949). It should be sung with vigour.

Timothy Dudley-Smith (b. 1926)

Words © Timothy Dudley-Smith. Used by permission.

96 The angel Gabriel from heaven came
(Gabriel's Message) Basque Noël

1 The angel Gabriel from heaven came,
His wings as drifted snow, his eyes as flame;
'All hail', said he, 'thou lowly maiden Mary,

    Most highly favour'd lady,
    Gloria!

2 'For known a blessèd Mother thou shalt be,
All generations laud and honour thee,
Thy Son shall be Emmanuel, by seers foretold,

    Most highly favour'd lady,
    Gloria!'

3 Then gentle Mary meekly bowed her head,
'To me be as it pleaseth God', she said,
'My soul shall laud and magnify his holy name.'

    Most highly favour'd lady,
    Gloria!

4 Of her Emmanuel, the Christ, was born
In Bethlehem, all on a Christmas morn,
And Christian folk throughout the world will ever say:

    'Most highly favour'd lady,
    Gloria!'

A carol from the prolific pen of Sabine Baring-Gould (see 'Sing lullaby!', no. 92), who was also a collector of folk-songs.
The tune is an arrangement by C. E. Pettiman (1866–1943) of a Basque noël.

Sabine Baring-Gould (1834–1924)

Words © in this version Words & Music/Jubilate Hymns.
Musical arrangement © 1922 B. Feldman & Co. Ltd, trading as H. Freeman & Co., London WC2H 0EA.

97. The first good joy that Mary had (The Seven Joys of Mary)

1. The first good joy that Mary had,
   It was the joy of one;
   To see the blessèd Jesus Christ
   When he was first her son.
   When he was first her son, Good Lord;

   And happy may we be;
   Praise Father, Son and Holy Ghost
   To all eternity.

2. The next good joy that Mary had,
   It was the joy of two;
   To see her own son Jesus Christ
   Making the lame to go.
   Making the lame to go, Good Lord;

   And happy may we be; . . .

3. The next good joy that Mary had,
   It was the joy of three;
   To see her own son Jesus Christ
   Making the blind to see.
   Making the blind to see, Good Lord;

   And happy may we be; . . .

4. The next good joy that Mary had,
   It was the joy of four;
   To see her own son Jesus Christ
   Reading the Bible o'er.
   Reading the Bible o'er, Good Lord;

   And happy may we be; . . .

5 The next good joy that Mary had,
It was the joy of five;
To see her own son Jesus Christ
Raising the dead to life.
Raising the dead to life, Good Lord;

    And happy may we be; . . .

6 The next good joy that Mary had,
It was the joy of six;
To see her own son Jesus Christ
Upon the crucifix.
Upon the crucifix, Good Lord;

    And happy may we be; . . .

7 The next good joy that Mary had,
It was the joy of seven;
To see her own son Jesus Christ
Ascending into heaven.
Ascending into heaven, Good Lord;

    And happy may we be; . . .

Sometimes called 'Joys Seven', this is another very popular folk carol, printed on broadsheets and sung all over 18th-and 19th-century England.

W. J. Phillips, in Carols, *wrote that he remembered in 1850 seeing the unemployed tramping through the London snow with shovels, singing to this tune 'We've got no work to do-oo-oo'.*

English traditional

98 *The first Nowell the angel did say* The First Nowell

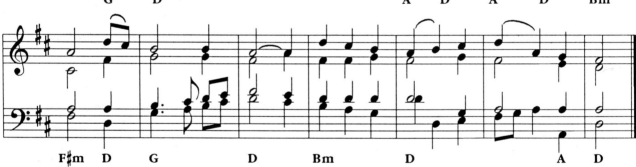

1 The first Nowell the angel did say
 Was to certain poor shepherds in fields as they lay;
 In fields where they lay, keeping their sheep,
 On a cold winter's night that was so deep:

  Nowell, Nowell, Nowell, Nowell,
  Born is the King of Israel.

2 They lookèd up and saw a star,
 Shining in the East, beyond them far:
 And to the earth it gave great light,
 And so it continued both day and night:

  Nowell, Nowell, Nowell, Nowell, . . .

3 And by the light of that same star,
 Three wise men came from country far;
 To seek for a king was their intent,
 And to follow the star wheresoever it went:

  Nowell, Nowell, Nowell, Nowell, . . .

4 This star drew nigh to the North-west;
 O'er Bethlehem it took its rest,
 And there it did both stop and stay
 Right over the place where Jesus lay:

  Nowell, Nowell, Nowell, Nowell, . . .

5 Then entered in those wise men three,
 Full reverently upon their knee,
 And offered there in his presence
 Both gold and myrrh and frankincense:

  Nowell, Nowell, Nowell, Nowell, . . .

6 Then let us all with one accord
 Sing praises to our heavenly Lord,
 That hath made heaven and earth of naught,
 And with his blood humankind hath bought:

  Nowell, Nowell, Nowell, Nowell, . . .

'Nowell', the old English form of the French noël, is a traditional expression of joy at the birth of Jesus. The carol tells the whole of the Christmas story, combining both Luke and Matthew.

The tune is so familiar and well-loved, few people realize how very peculiar it is. It has been suggested that it might originally have been a descant to a tune that has been lost.

English traditional

99 The great God of heaven is come down to earth — A Virgin Unspotted

1 The great God of heaven is come down to earth,
His mother a virgin, and sinless his birth;
The Father eternal his Father alone:
He sleeps in the manger; he reigns on the throne:

    Then let us adore him, and praise his great love:
    To save us poor sinners he came from above.

2 A babe on the breast of a maiden he lies,
Yet sits with the Father on high in the skies;
Before him their faces the seraphim hide,
While Joseph stands waiting, unscared, by his side:

    Then let us adore him, and praise his great love; . . .

3 Lo! here is Emmanuel, here is the Child,
The Son that was promised to Mary so mild;
Whose power and dominion shall ever increase,
The Prince that shall rule o'er a kingdom of peace:

    Then let us adore him, and praise his great love: . . .

4 The Wonderful Counsellor, boundless in might,
The Father's own image, the beam of his light;
Behold him now wearing the likeness of man,
Weak, helpless, and speechless, in measure a span:

    Then let us adore him, and praise his great love: . . .

5 O wonder of wonders, which none can unfold:
The Ancient of days is an hour or two old;
The Maker of all things is made of the earth,
Child is worshipped by angels, and God comes to birth:

    Then let us adore him, and praise his great love: . . .

A carol with magnificent words, using a series of striking contrasts to emphasize the difference between God's awesome greatness and the frail helplessness of the little human baby that contains him: 'The Ancient of days is an hour or two old'.

'A Virgin Unspotted' is a traditional English folk carol tune. It can be effective to sing one or more verses solo.

Henry Ramsden Bramley (1833–1917)

100 The holly and the ivy — English traditional melody

1 The holly and the ivy,
 When they are both full grown,
 Of all the trees that are in the wood,
 The holly bears the crown:

  O, the rising of the sun
  And the running of the deer,
  The playing of the merry organ,
  Sweet singing in the choir.

2 The holly bears a blossom,
 As white as the lily flower,
 And Mary bore sweet Jesus Christ,
 To be our sweet Saviour:

  O, the rising of the sun . . .

3 The holly bears a berry,
 As red as any blood,
 And Mary bore sweet Jesus Christ,
 To do poor sinners good:

  O, the rising of the sun . . .

4 The holly bears a prickle,
 As sharp as any thorn,
 And Mary bore sweet Jesus Christ
 On Christmas Day in the morn:

  O, the rising of the sun . . .

5 The holly bears a bark,
 As bitter as any gall,
 And Mary bore sweet Jesus Christ
 For to redeem us all:

  O, the rising of the sun . . .

6 The holly and the ivy,
 When they are both full grown,
 Of all the trees that are in the wood,
 The holly bears the crown:

  O, the rising of the sun . . .

A very old folk carol, which Cecil Sharp collected in Chipping Campden, and a reminder that 'carol' originally meant a dance accompanied with singing. It was probably pagan in origin, the holly symbolizing the masculine, and the ivy the feminine elements, and the whole being sung as a dance between the men and the women.

English traditional, collected by Cecil Sharp (1859–1924)

101 *The people that in darkness sat* Dundee

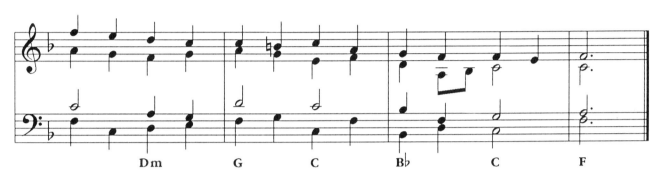

1. The people that in darkness sat
   A glorious light have seen;
   The light has shined on them who long
   In shades of death have been.

2. To hail thee, Son of Righteousness,
   The gathering nations come;
   They joy as when the reapers bear
   Their harvest treasures home.

3. For thou their burden dost remove,
   And break the tyrant's rod,
   As in the day when Midian fell
   Before the sword of God.

4. For unto us a child is born,
   To us a son is given,
   And on his shoulder ever rests
   All power in earth and heaven.

5. His name shall be the Prince of Peace,
   The everlasting Lord,
   The Wonderful, the Counsellor,
   The God by all adored.

6. His righteous government and power
   Shall over all extend;
   On judgement and on justice based,
   His reign shall have no end.

7. Lord Jesus, reign in us, we pray,
   And make us thine alone,
   Who with the Father ever art
   And Holy Spirit One.

*A paraphrase of Isaiah 9.2–7, ending with a prayer.
'Dundee', sometimes known as 'French', is one of the
most popular and satisfying of all the Scottish metrical
psalm tunes, which owe their effectiveness to their
simplicity.*

Scottish Paraphrases *1781, originally J. Morrison
(1750–98), revised*

102 There'll be a new world beginnin' from tonight
(Cowboy Carol)

There'll be a new world beginnin' from tonight!
There'll be a new world beginnin' from tonight!
When I climb up to my saddle,
Gonna take him to my heart!
There'll be a new world beginnin' from tonight!

1 Right across the prairie,
  Clear across the valley,
  Straight across every heart and hand,
  There'll be a right new brand of livin'
  That'll sweep like lightnin' fire
  And take away the hate from every land.

   There'll be a new world beginnin' from tonight! . . .

2 Yoi, yippee! We're gonna ride the trail!
  Yoi, yippee! We're gonna ride today!
  When I climb up to my saddle,
  Gonna take him to my heart!
  There'll be a new world beginnin' from tonight,
  From tonight!

A Moral Rearmament carol, based on the old ay-ay-yippee cowboy trail songs. It has become popular as one of the high points of the famous annual carol concert in the Royal Festival Hall, given by doctors and nurses from London hospitals to raise money for the Malcolm Sargent Cancer Fund for Children.

Coconut shells might provide an appropriate accompaniment!

Cecil Broadhurst

Words and music © 1949 The Oxford Group, 12 Palace Street, London SW1E 5JF.

103

***There's a star in the east on Christmas morn
(Rise up, Shepherd)***

1 There's a star in the east on Christmas morn,
    Rise up, shepherd, and follow.
  It will lead to the place where the Saviour's born,
    Rise up, shepherd, and follow.

   Leave your sheep and leave your lambs,
     Rise up, shepherd, and follow;
   Leave your ewes and leave your rams,
     Rise up, shepherd, and follow.
   Follow, follow,
     Rise up, shepherd, and follow,
   Follow the star of Bethlehem,
     Rise up, shepherd, and follow.

2 If you take good heed to the angel's words,
    Rise up, shepherd, and follow,
  You'll forget your flocks, you'll forget your herds;
    Rise up, shepherd, and follow.

   Leave your sheep and leave your lambs, . . .

We might have printed 'foller' instead of 'follow': there is no doubt that the first spelling is closer to the spirit of the piece.

American traditional.

104 *The virgin Mary had a baby boy*   The Virgin Mary

1. The virgin Mary had a baby boy,
   The virgin Mary had a baby boy,
   The virgin Mary had a baby boy
   And they say that his name was Jesus.

   He come from the glory,
   He come from the glorious kingdom;
   (Yes!) he come from the glory,
   He come from the glorious kingdom:
   O yes, believer!
   O yes, believer!
   He come from the glory,
   He come from the glorious kingdom.

2. The angels sang when the baby was born,
   The angels sang when the baby was born,
   The angels sang when the baby was born
   And they sang that his name was Jesus.

   He come from the glory, ...

3. The shepherds came where the baby was born,
   The shepherds came where the baby was born,
   The shepherds came where the baby was born
   And they say that his name was Jesus.

   He come from the glory, ...

A calypso is a West Indian ballad, sometimes satirical, always topical, usually extemporized to a percussive syncopated accompaniment. In this case it is the story of Jesus' birth that is treated as a piece of topical news.

West Indian traditional

Words and music from the Edric Connor Collection © 1945 Boosey & Co. Ltd. Used by permission.

105 This is the truth sent from above
(The Truth from Above) English traditional melody

1. This is the truth sent from above,
   The truth of God, the God of love,
   Therefore don't turn me from your door,
   But hearken all both rich and poor.

2. The first thing which I do relate
   Is that God did man create;
   The next thing which to you I'll tell
   Woman was made with man to dwell.

3. Thus we were heirs to endless woes,
   Till God the Lord did interpose;
   And so a promise soon did run
   That he would redeem us by his son.

4. And at that season of the year
   Our blest Redeemer did appear;
   He here did live, and here did preach,
   And many thousands he did teach.

5. Thus he in love to us behaved,
   To show us how we must be saved;
   And if you want to know the way,
   Be pleased to hear what he did say.

A challenging carol musically, this is very haunting and effective in performance, especially as an opening number. Try having a soloist for verse 1, and have your church or hall in complete darkness, gradually increasing the light either by candle power or dimmer switch.

English traditional, collected by Ralph Vaughan Williams (1872–1958)

Music © Stainer & Bell. Used by permission.

106 'Twas in the moon of wintertime — Une Jeune Pucelle

1. 'Twas in the moon of wintertime,
   When all the birds had fled,
   That God the Lord of all the earth
   Sent angel-choirs instead;
   Before their light the stars grew dim,
   And wondering hunters heard the hymn:

   Jesus your king is born,
   Jesus is born,
   In excelsis gloria.

2. Within a lodge of broken bark
   The tender babe was found;
   A ragged robe of rabbit skin
   Enwrapped his beauty round:
   But as the hunter braves drew nigh,
   The angel-song rang loud and high:

   Jesus your king is born, . . .

3. The earliest moon of wintertime
   Is not so round and fair
   As was the ring of glory on
   The helpless infant there.
   The chiefs from far before him knelt
   With gifts of fox and beaver-pelt.

   Jesus your king is born, . . .

4. O children of the forest free,
   The angel song is true;
   The holy child of earth and heaven
   Is born today for you.
   Come kneel before the radiant boy,
   Who brings you beauty, peace, and joy.

   Jesus your king is born, . . .

A carol in which the stable is visited by North American Indian hunters and braves. Its many references to the natural world evoke a strong and distinctive atmosphere.

The traditional French tune, 'Une Jeune Pucelle', has been harmonized here by Frederick Jackisch (b. 1922). A light percussion accompaniment would work well.

Jesse Edgar Middleton (1872–1960)

107 Unto us a boy is born! Puer Nobis

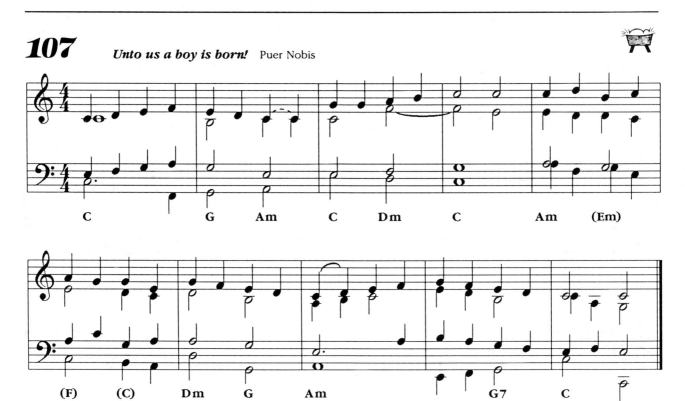

1 Unto us a boy is born!
 King of all creation,
 Came he to the world forlorn,
 The Lord of every nation, the Lord of every nation.

2 Cradled in a stall was he
 With sleepy cows and asses;
 But the very beasts could see
 That he all men surpasses, that he all men surpasses.

3 Herod then with fear was filled:
 'A prince', he said, 'in Jewry!'
 All the little boys he killed
 At Bethlem in his fury, at Bethlem in his fury.

4 Now may Mary's son, who came
 So long ago to love us,
 Lead us all with hearts aflame
 Unto the joys above us, unto the joys above us.

5 Omega and Alpha he!
 Let the organ thunder,
 While the choir with peals of glee
 Doth rend the air asunder, doth rend the air asunder.

You really need some good strong voices to make this one go, to carry the 'Herod then with fear was filled' verse, and an organ that can really 'thunder' also adds to the effect.

The melody, 'Puer Nobis', is in the Piae Cantiones *of 1582, from which so many carol tunes have been taken. The harmony is by G. H. Palmer (1846–1926).*

Latin, 15th century, tr. Percy Dearmer (1867–1936)

1 Wake, O wake! with tidings thrilling
   The watchmen all the air are filling,
   Arise, Jerusalem, arise!
   Midnight strikes! no more delaying,
   'The hour has come!' we hear them saying.
   Where are ye all, ye virgins wise?
   The Bridegroom comes in sight,
   Raise high your torches bright!
   Alleluya!
   The wedding song
   Swells loud and strong:
   Go forth and join the festal throng.

2 Sion hears the watchmen shouting,
   Her heart leaps up with joy undoubting,
   She stands and waits with eager eyes;
   See her Friend from heaven descending,
   Adorned with truth and grace unending!
   Her light burns clear, her star doth rise.
   Now come, thou precious Crown,
   Lord Jesu, God's own Son!
   Hosanna!
   Let us prepare
   To follow there,
   Where in thy supper we may share.

3 Every soul in thee rejoices;
   From earthly and angelic voices
   Be glory given to thee alone!
   Now the gates of pearl receive us,
   Thy presence never more shall leave us,
   We stand with angels round thy throne.
   Earth cannot give below
   The bliss thou dost bestow.
   Alleluya!
   Grant us to raise,
   To length of days,
   The triumph-chorus of thy praise.

The stirring words, and J. S. Bach's triumphant chorale arrangement 'Sleepers, Wake' of Nicolai's tune 'Wachet Auf', make this one of the grandest carols in any collection. The words and original melody were written at the time of a terrible plague in 1597, and are the fruit of Pastor Philipp Nicolai's profound meditations on the doctrine of eternal life, after 1,300 of his own parishioners had perished. The main biblical references are to Matthew 25, the parable of the wise and foolish virgins.

Philipp Nicolai (1556–1608), tr. F. C. Birkit (1864–1935)

109 We three kings of Orient are — Kings of Orient

(The Kings)
1. We three kings of Orient are;
   Bearing gifts we traverse afar
   Field and fountain, moor and mountain,
   Following yonder star:

   O star of wonder, star of night,
   Star with royal beauty bright,
   Westward leading, still proceeding,
   Guide us to thy perfect light.

(Caspar)
2. Born a king on Bethlehem plain
   Gold I bring, to crown him again —
   King for ever, ceasing never,
   Over us all to reign:

   O star of wonder, star of night, . . .

(Melchior)
3. Frankincense to offer have I;
   Incense owns a deity nigh:
   Prayer and praising, all are raising,
   Worship him, God most high:

   O star of wonder, star of night, . . .

(Balthazar)
4. Myrrh is mine: its bitter perfume
   Breathes a life of gathering gloom;
   Sorrowing, sighing, bleeding, dying,
   Sealed in the stone-cold tomb:

   O star of wonder, star of night, . . .

(All)
5 Glorious now, behold him arise,
   King, and God, and sacrifice!
   Heaven sings alleluya,
   Alleluya the earth replies:

   O star of wonder, star of night, . . .

John Henry Hopkins Jr

A very successful Victorian carol — it was written in 1857 — that works very well when staged dramatically: the three kings, Caspar, Melchior and Balthazar, entering in procession singing the first verse, then each singing a solo verse, with the whole congregation joining in the choruses.

110 We wish you a merry Christmas
(A Merry Christmas)   English traditional melody

1 We wish you a merry Christmas,
   We wish you a merry Christmas,
   We wish you a merry Christmas
   And a happy New Year.

   Good tidings we bring
   To you and your kin;
   We wish you a merry Christmas
   And a happy New Year.

2 Now bring us some figgy pudding,
   Now bring us some figgy pudding,
   Now bring us some figgy pudding
   And bring some out here.

   Good tidings we bring . . .

3 For we all like figgy pudding,
   For we all like figgy pudding,
   For we all like figgy pudding,
   So bring some out here.

   Good tidings we bring . . .

4 And we won't go until we've got some,
   And we won't go until we've got some,
   And we won't go until we've got some,
   So bring some out here.

   Good tidings we bring . . .

A secular carol, very popular with house-to-house carol singers as a finale — or until the hint is taken. It's worth noting that the chorus begins 'Good tidings we bring to you and your <u>kin</u>', i.e. your family, not your <u>king</u>, which is often sung in error, possibly misread by poor torch light, and because it rhymes with 'bring'.

English West Country traditional

111 What child is this, who laid to rest — Greensleeves

1 What child is this, who laid to rest
  On Mary's lap is sleeping?
  Whom angels greet with anthems sweet,
  While shepherds watch are keeping?
  This, this is Christ the King,
  Whom shepherds worship and angels sing:
  Haste, haste to bring him praise
  The Babe, the son of Mary.

2 Why lies he in such mean estate,
  Where ox and ass are feeding?
  Come, have no fear, God's son is here,
  His love all loves exceeding:
  Nails, spear, shall pierce him through,
  The cross be borne for me, for you:
  Hail, hail, the Saviour comes,
  The Babe, the son of Mary.

3 So bring him incense, gold and myrrh,
  All tongues and peoples own him,
  The King of Kings salvation brings,
  Let every heart enthrone him:
  Raise, raise your song on high
  While Mary sings a lullaby,
  Joy, joy, for Christ is born,
  The Babe, the son of Mary.

The Christmas story told again, in question and answer form, this time to the well-known traditional English melody 'Greensleeves', sometimes attributed to Henry VIII, and harmonized here by C. H. Dearnley.

W. Chatterton Dix (1837–98) and others

Words adapted for English Praise 1975. *Used by permission of Oxford University Press.*
Music arr. Christopher Dearnley (b. 1930), from English Praise 1975. *Used by permission of Oxford University Press.*

112 *While shepherds watched their flocks by night* Winchester Old

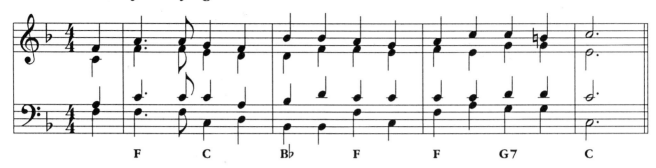

1. While shepherds watched their flocks by night,
   All seated on the ground,
   The angel of the Lord came down,
   And glory shone around.

2. 'Fear not', said he (for mighty dread
   Had seized their troubled mind);
   'Glad tidings of great joy I bring
   To you and humankind.

3. 'To you in David's town this day
   Is born of David's line
   A Saviour, who is Christ the Lord;
   And this shall be the sign:

4. 'The heavenly Babe you there shall find
   To human view displayed,
   All meanly wrapped in swathing bands,
   And in a manger laid.'

5. Thus spake the seraph; and forthwith
   Appeared a shining throng
   Of angels praising God, who thus
   Addressed their joyful song:

6. 'All glory be to God on high,
   And on the earth be peace;
   Good-will henceforth from heaven to earth
   Begin and never cease.'

Biblical paraphrasing at its best, by the Poet Laureate of his day, Nahum Tate. It is a paraphrase of the Nativity story in Luke 2.8–14, and while respecting the text, the poet has turned the story into simple, clear, singable verse.

The tune is 'Winchester Old', first published in Thomas Este's Psalter (1592).

Nahum Tate (1652–1715)

113 *Will you come and see the light?* Kelvingrove

1. Will you come and see the light from the stable door?
   It is shining newly bright, though it shone before.
   It will be your guiding star, it will show you who you are.
   Will you hide, or decide to meet the light?

2. Will you step into the light that can free the slave?
   It will stand for what is right, it will heal and save.
   By the pyramids of greed there's a longing to be freed.
   Will you hide, or decide to meet the light?

3. Will you tell about the light in the prison cell?
   Though it's shackled out of sight, it is shining well.
   When the truth is cut and bruised, and the innocent abused,
   Will you hide, or decide to meet the light?

4. Will you join the hope alight in a young girl's eyes
   Of the mighty put to flight by a baby's cries?
   When the lowest and the least are the foremost at the feast,
   Will you hide, or decide to meet the light?

5. Will you travel by the light of the babe new born?
   In the candle lit at night there's a gleam of dawn,
   And the darkness all about is too dim to put it out:
   Will you hide, or decide to meet the light?

Written for Christian Aid's 'God with Us' booklet, for the Advent Candle Ceremony.

The Scottish traditional melody 'Kelvingrove' has been arranged for this carol by Valerie Ruddle.

Brian Wren

Words © Brian Wren 1989. Used by permission of Oxford University Press.

Arrangement © Valerie Ruddle. Used by permission.

Index of First Lines and Titles

A child this day is born	1
A cry in the night	2
A great and mighty wonder	3
All my heart this night rejoices	4
Angels, from the realms of glory	5
As Joseph was a-walking	6
As with gladness	7
A virgin most pure	8
Away in a manger	9
Ballad of the Homeless Christ	2
Bethlehem, of noble cities	10
Born in the night	11
Brightest and best	12
Calypso Carol	89
Cherry Tree Carol	7
Child in the manger	13
Child of Mary, newly born	14
Christians awake!	15
Come, come, come to the manger	16
Come, they told me	17
Come, thou long-expected Jesus	18
Coventry Carol	65
Cowboy Carol	102
Dans cette étable	19
Deck the hall	20
Deep peace	21
Ding-dong, ding	22
Ding dong merrily on high	23
Every star shall sing a carol	24
Gabriel's Message	96
Gaelic Blessing, A	21
Gallery Carol	87
Georgie	42
Girls and boys, leave your toys	25
Gloria, gloria in excelsis Deo	26
God rest ye merry	27
Good Enough for Him	54
Good King Wenceslas	28
Go, tell it on the mountain	29
Hail, Mary, full of grace	30
Hail to the Lord's Anointed!	31
Hark! a herald voice	32
Hark, the glad sound!	33
Hark! the herald angels sing	34
Here we go up to Bethlehem	35
He smiles within his cradle	36
Hills of the North, rejoice	37
Holy Child	38
How brightly shines the Morning Star	39
How lovely on the mountains	40
Il est né le divin enfant	41
I'm standing at windows	42
In a byre near Bethlehem	43
In dulci jubilo	44
Infant holy, infant lowly	45
Infant King, The	92
In the bleak midwinter	46
I saw three ships	47
It came upon the midnight clear	48
It was on a starry night	49
I warm my son upon my breast	50
I wonder as I wander	51
Jesus, good above all other	52
Jesus, Son of God	53
Jesus was born in a stable	54
Joseph, dearest Joseph mine	55
Joy to the world	56
King Jesus hath a garden	57
Les anges dans nos campagnes	58
Light, scattering the darkness	59
Little donkey	60
Little Drummer, The	17
Little Jesus, sweetly sleep	61
Lo! he comes with clouds descending	62
Long time ago in Bethlehem	63
Lourdes Hymn	79
Love came down at Christmas	64
Lully, lulla, thou little tiny child	65
Magnificat anima mea dominum	66
Make straight in the desert	67
Make way, make way	68
Mary had a baby	69
Mary's Boy-Child	63
Masters in this hall	70
Merry Christmas, A	110
Nkosi Jesus	50
No crowded eastern street	71
Now the holly bears a berry	72
O come, all ye faithful	73
O come, O come, Emmanuel	74
Of the Father's heart begotten	75
O leave your sheep	76
O little one sweet	77
O little town of Bethlehem	78
O Mary most holy	79
Once in royal David's city	80
On Christmas night, all Christians sing	81
On Jordan's bank	82
O Tannenbaum!	83
Our God Reigns	40
O worship the Lord in the beauty of holiness!	84
Past three a clock	85
People, look East	86
Rejoice and be merry	87
Rise up, Shepherd	103
Rocking	61
Sans Day Carol	72
See amid the winter's snow	88
See him lying on a bed of straw	89
Seven Joys of Mary, The	97
Shepherds in the field abiding	90
Silent night	91
Sing lullaby!	92
Sing this night	93
Star Carol	93
Starry Night, A	49
Stille Nacht	94
Sussex Carol	81
Tell out, my soul	95
The angel Gabriel	96
The first good joy that Mary had	97
The first Nowell	98
The great God of heaven	99
The holly and the ivy	100
The people that in darkness sat	101
There'll be a new world	102
There's a star in the east	103
The virgin Mary had a baby boy	104
This is the truth sent from above	105
Truth from Above, The	105
'Twas in the moon of wintertime	106
Unto us a boy is born!	107
Up! good Christen folk	22
Wake, O wake!	108
We three kings	109
We wish you a merry Christmas	110
What child is this	111
While shepherds watched	112
Will you come and see the light?	113
Word of Life, The	43
Zither Carol	25

Subject Index

Advent 18, 30, 31, 32, 40, 62, 66, 67, 68, 74, 82, 86, 101, 108
angels 1, 5, 6, 8, 16, 32, 33, 34, 44, 46, 47, 49, 58, 63, 72, 87, 96
annunciation 30, 79, 96
bells 22, 23, 44, 45, 49, 60
Bethlehem 10, 35, 53, 78, 89
blessing 21
celebration 20, 22, 23, 24, 25, 26, 27, 41, 44, 47, 48, 50, 56, 57, 73, 81, 85, 87, 90, 93, 98, 107
children 9, 16, 17, 25, 29, 30, 35, 42, 50, 51, 52, 60, 61, 66, 69, 78, 89, 91, 96, 103, 104, 109, 110
creation 21, 24, 39, 75, 105
Epiphany 7, 10, 12, 31, 59, 84, 87, 101, 109
good news 29, 30, 31, 37, 40, 45, 55, 66, 70, 94, 102
grace 38
Herod 65, 67, 107
Holy Innocents 65, 67, 107
homelessness 2, 11, 51, 54
incarnation 3, 8, 34, 39, 46, 51, 64, 70, 75, 78, 80, 88, 99, 106
John the Baptist 67, 81
Joseph 6, 55
lament 92
liberation 31, 33, 58, 66, 68, 82
life of Jesus 2, 11, 14, 24, 43, 51, 62, 67, 92, 100, 111
light 11, 12, 14, 21, 32, 36, 39, 59, 81, 91, 94, 101, 108, 113
Magnificat 66, 95
Mary 11, 30, 50, 60, 63, 66, 79, 95, 96, 97, 100, 104
nations 3, 5, 18, 31, 37, 40, 56, 59
outcasts 13, 42
peace 21, 31, 48, 49
poverty 17, 27, 42, 51, 66, 89, 95, 113
promise and prophecy 5, 13, 31, 38, 48, 51, 67, 74, 75, 76, 88, 99, 101
redemption 3, 5, 8, 11, 12, 13, 14, 15, 18, 19, 31, 32, 34, 38, 44, 48, 51, 63, 72, 78, 79, 81, 88, 91, 94, 105
response 4, 7, 9, 12, 15, 32, 36, 46, 50, 56, 57, 67, 68, 73, 84, 85, 89, 93, 106
salvation 82, 87, 89, 91, 105
seasonal 20, 28, 83, 86, 100, 106, 110
shepherds 1, 8, 29, 49, 58, 70, 78, 90, 103, 111, 112
stable 4, 6, 9, 16, 17, 19, 25, 36, 38, 41, 43, 45, 46, 51, 54, 55, 61, 76, 77, 80, 89, 91, 92, 94, 106, 111
story telling 1, 5, 8, 15, 25, 27, 47, 63, 69, 70, 73, 80, 85, 87, 88, 93, 98, 104, 107, 112
titles of Christ 14, 34, 39, 74, 99, 101
triumph 39, 40, 56, 62, 92, 108
wise men 5, 7, 31, 41, 76, 87, 109
word of life 43
worship 5, 10, 12, 25, 26, 73, 75, 84, 99, 108, 109, 111, 112

Silent night, holy night!
From the heav'ns' golden height
Comes salvation to all here below!
Love and kindness to all let us show!
Christ is born one of us!
Christ is born one of us!

Silent night, holy night!
God pours down, full of might,
Father's love on the whole human race,
Yet as brother is glad to embrace
Jesus, born for us all!
Jesus, born for us all!

Silent night, holy night!
Ancient wrong now made right!
Prophets' words are now coming true!
God has done what he promised to do –
Care for all the world,
Care for all the world!

A new translation of the three additional verses of 'Silent night', (no. 91) discovered in 1997.

Fiona McKenzie © Mowbray, a Cassell imprint, 1998